S0-CEZ-846

ON THE DRAGON HILLS

ON
THE
DRAGON
HILLS

BY

Roy S. Lautenschlager

THE WESTMINSTER PRESS
Philadelphia

COPYRIGHT © MCMLXX THE WESTMINSTER PRESS

All rights reserved—no part of this book may be reproduced in any form without permission in writing from the publisher, except by a reviewer who wishes to quote brief passages in connection with a review in magazine or newspaper.

STANDARD BOOK NO. 664-20884-3
LIBRARY OF CONGRESS CATALOG CARD NO. 72-98382

Grateful acknowledgment is made to Coward-McCann for permission to use lines from *The White Cliffs,* by Alice Duer Miller.

Published by The Westminster Press ®
Philadelphia, Pennsylvania

PRINTED IN THE UNITED STATES OF AMERICA

To the grandchildren—
Laura, Warren, and Andrew

CONTENTS

CONTENTS

FOREWORD

Several years ago I started with the idea of writing a sketch for my grandchildren, covering experiences and observations in connection with my nearly thirty years of Mission service in China (1922–1951). Later it seemed expedient to produce a broader account for the interest of the general reader. My theme may be stated as the role of an educational missionary in the throes of revolutions and wars, and my purpose is to perpetuate the precious bonds of Christian fellowship.

In producing this compound of biography and events, I have not undertaken so much to give a systematic history as to present personal experiences and reactions in particular situations and times.

My primary source material has consisted of stacks of preserved family letters written from China throughout three decades. From these have come the specifics and personal touches of the narrative. They also provided the general outline for the march of events.

Besides these descriptive letters, I have been favored with full access to a mass of pamphlets, documents, and personal writings of several fellow missionaries. They covered a broad scope: origin of Presbyterian Missions in East China, the city of Hangchow and the opening of Christian work there, the beginning of the Presbyterian college—

with numerous of its annual reports throughout the years. For this wealth of material I am particularly indebted to the late Dr. Elmer L. Mattox and Mrs. Kepler Van Evera, who generously made available their collections (now preserved in the Presbyterian Historical Society archives, Philadelphia). In addition, the late Dr. R. J. McMullen lent me his bound collection of letters relating to the Japanese occupation of Hangchow, for which help I am grateful.

R. S. L.

Wooster, Ohio

I

THE LURE OF HANGCHOW

*W*E CALLED IT our honeymoon voyage, Grace and I did. Two well-filled years had slipped by since marriage—adding up to each a master's degree from the University of Michigan and a clarified concept of our common vocation and personal commissions to serve in China as Christian educators.

In Vancouver the *bon voyage* streamers fluttered gaily, then gently snapped. We were off! It was September 7, 1922, on the S.S. *Empress of Russia,* first-class. The vast waters of the Pacific stretched before us, and beyond stood the challenge of an ancient civilization newly awakened. Within us bloomed ideals and hopes founded upon the sense of a fruitful togetherness under the Guiding Hand. Our lifework in spiritual adventure was launched.

The appeals of China as a field for Christian witness and service were manifold; to us particularly so, since they sounded the call for modern education. Assignment: Hangchow Christian College! The door had opened. Our interest had been directly fed by enthusiastic reports from my brother Stanton and wife, Sarah, already for the past two years stationed in North China (Chefoo, Shantung). We became impressed by the rich heritage of China's ancient culture, the high esteem for the scholar (teacher), the apparent yearning for scientific knowledge and its application to social and political institutions. All this spelled out need and opportunity in capital letters. But yet deeper, the word came ringing forth: "China is wide open for the gospel." We consequently envisioned the natural, indirect process of student evangelism and the training of Christian leadership. For only upon the groundwork of Christian faith and by its spiritual motivation, we believed, could the old civilization be reborn. Notably, also, barely a decade back the Imperial structure of long ages had collapsed and the Republic of China had been born—founded by the spirit and guiding hand of the Christian revolutionist, Dr. Sun Yat-sen.

On schedule, the eleventh day brought us to port (Yokohama) and offered the first taste of Asiatic life. A melee of humanity in odd garb and clattering sandals surrounded us, chattering strangely. How enticing the open-fronted shops with their dainty silks, porcelains, and pearls; and what a treat to obtain by auto ride a few glimpses of Imperial Tokyo! Surely the Japanese showed themselves as a people of keen enterprise, rare artistic temperament, and habitual courtesy. We had a gay and glittering evening at the port of Kobe, and then a day's stop for refueling at Nagasaki, where all the coal was handled in baskets by plucky Japanese women.

"Now two days to Shanghai," came the exciting word. Ship's crew and stewards changed garb, replacing blue with dazzling white. Choppy waters, losing their ocean green, turned a murky coastal yellow, and presently the China Sea was offering a sample of the humid and silt-laden Yangtze delta. Then, our approach to the famed international city, apart from the thrill of arrival, afforded disappointingly few attractions. Due to low tide, we docked far out at the Whangpoo wharf, requiring a ten-mile trip by "tender service" after debarkation. Finally appeared the imposing frontage of the International Settlement, and elatedly we set foot (though unsteadily) on the stable foundations of the Shanghai Bund. It was then September 22, 1922.

"Welcome to China and greetings from Hangchow Christian College." This salutation was heartily accorded by Edward Evans, professor of physics, who, being native-born, knew the city well and rattled off its lingo. Obligingly and competently he took us in tow. "Time is pressing," he urged. "Classes are waiting. We shall swish off for Hangchow tomorrow noon."

What a hubbub and clamor of ricksha pullers! Settled in and with baggage piled high on us, we arrived shortly thereafter at first base. It was the renowned and accommodating Shanghai Missionary Home, founded in earlier times by Edward's parents. Our next priority was to report at the all-China administrative offices of the Presbyterian Mission. Indeed, making the acquaintance of Dr. Walter M. Lowrie, esteemed China Secretary, and Rev. Charles M. Myers, efficient head of the Associated Missions Treasurers, brought us the warmhearted touch of key personalities in the fields of policy and finance.

Then came the adventure of trying it on our own. Along with the language problem arose the puzzle of handling money—so much of it! In exchange for the local silver dollar, known as "Mexican" (rated at two to one U.S.), I acquired an amazing amount of small coin. What a new-found prosperity to be loaded with three hundred pennies or even twenty dimes! At least the situation called for a stout and sizable coin bag. The real excitement occurred when a ricksha puller dashed off with Grace as she failed to recognize the service door of the Home. Frantically I ran after them, shouting, "Stop! Stop!" Then the laugh turned on us—all in that wonderful universal language.

On the afternoon of the following day the Shanghai-Hangchow train served to complete our travel (doing 120 miles in five hours and opening the first joyous opportunity to glimpse the real China). From our coach windows, rich rice fields, irrigation canals, scattered villages, walled towns, and occasional pagodas began to provide the pattern of society stretched over the level landscape. Within we felt an atmosphere of leisure and friendliness, as fellow passengers, all Chinese, chatted ceaselessly while sipping tea from handleless cups. Traveling in style on leather upholstered seats, first-class (there being also second and third), these could be taken for prosperous businessmen or government functionaries. Several understood English; but our host introduced us in Chinese by stating the name as Lau-ten, which apparently by literal translation carried the idea of "labor and light." Thus we had our first lesson in this utterly strange language, along with acquiring the taste for green tea and salted watermelon seeds. A surprising and somewhat disconcerting aspect of train service was the regular pacing of armed guard through the coaches, suggesting the problem of order and safety.

Entering Hangchow, the train passed through a great gap in the ancient city wall, and it seemed as though this mighty, fire-spouting "iron dragon" had broken through its old seclusions and time-honored securities. At the main station, official welcome awaited. Dr. Elmer L. Mattox, acting president of the college, and Mrs. Mattox, both senior members of the Presbyterian group, graciously received us. And Mrs. Kepler Van Evera was there, whose acquaintanceship, along with that of her husband, we had enjoyed in Ann Arbor while they were on their furlough.

Again the train moved on, continuing another five miles to the railway terminal at Zakow, a remote suburb just a mile from the campus. By this time night had set in, shutting off from view the local surroundings.

Still a last lap of our journey remained, and it proved to be both arduous and mysterious. Now, in almost total darkness we had to follow a pathway along the river's edge, the men walking in front, ladies following in sedan chairs, and baggage swung on shoulder poles of luggage-bearing coolies. As our little entourage moved forward, night seemed to have swallowed us—while close to one side the unseen waters splashed and on the other rose the dim outline of rugged cliffs. I put my trust in Ed's guiding arm, while Grace, though alarmed, resigned herself to swinging along in her strange carriage. Behind us followed the rhythmic "hi-yo-ho" song of the coolies, giving cheerful assurance, but around us was only the dark and hushed unknown. Could nature and man have better contrived to enshroud the arriving stranger in mystery? This much we were told: A little more light was customary and had, of course, been intended, but by some oversight the usual bamboo torches just had not turned up.

Reaching the campus entrance at the base of the bluff, we still had not actually arrived; a further test awaited. Here a narrow and winding path of steep ascent brought us onto a broad and level area with large buildings. These we simply bypassed, and with more puffing we continued another upward stretch between rows of cryptomeria trees, finally reaching the Mattox residence. This was journey's end. We were to live with the Mattoxes for our first year. So here was home for the travel-weary: a warm fellowship, a hearty dinner, an inviting bed—and tomorrow a whole new world awaiting us at dawn.

Sunday morning raised us up, charged with the spirit of

curiosity. What would we find in this exalted setting of our new abode? Little by way of previous description had prepared us for it. In haste we stepped to the window to see —again the mystery! Mother Nature, reluctant to reveal her secrets, had dropped a tantalizing gray curtain of haze all around us. The entire hillside lay buried in a heavy fog. The Dragon Hills had their own intimate way of welcome, disclosing only gradually their innate qualities and magnificent surroundings.

The call of the breakfast gong brought us sprightly to the table, joining our hostess and host. An atmosphere of combined simplicity and formality immediately impressed us as inviting: linen table mats, shining brass finger bowls with accompanying fruit knives, a spacious platter of colorful contents as centerpiece, and standing stately off to the side, the table boy in starched white gown. What lay on the platter appeared to me like an array of lovely ripe tomatoes, which unfortunately was not exactly my favorite for breakfast. But surely one could learn to discipline and adapt one's tastes. Imagine my surprise when, by the example of the hostess, I sliced off the hood and discovered a supremely luscious persimmon. Already I was indulging in what proved to become my choice Chinese fruit. It turned out to be the height of the season for persimmons, Hangchow area's most abundant fruit. Later I could look upon this initiating experience as rather symbolic of the quick appeal of tastes and sights of things Chinese.

By now the surrounding haze offered sufficient transparency to provide a close-in view of our position, enabling us to fix our location in the midst of seven Western-type brick residences, perched on the edge of a sharply sloping hillside. About fifty feet below lay a sort of plateau, constituting the college quadrangle, upon which stood three large red-brick buildings and a neat gray-stone chapel. On the left, beyond a ravine, was a set of Chinese houses, while to the right, far below, lay the spread-out athletic field. Along the broad frontage flowed the expansive waters of the Chien Tang River, about to be entering the Hangchow Bay. Over this entire area vegetation stood lush: hedges and flowers abounding, long-armed camphor trees shading the lawns, and stately cryptomerias bordering the paths. We fell quickly under the charm of this wealth of natural beauty.

Soon the hour arrived when staff and students assembled for Sunday worship. This would be our first appearance before the community and an occasion for curiosity and scrutiny. For us there was also plenty to be curious about, as we sat for the first time under Scripture and sermon, hardly comprehending a word. With hymns it was different, since all carried familiar tunes that we could hum or sing along with in our own language. Finally, quite unmistakably came the two-syllable word that pronounced the welcome *"Ya-men."* The lovely chapel, with its hand-pumped pipe organ, was well set at the heart of the campus, and its message was acknowledged as the spirit of the community.

As accepted members of the family, yet totally unfamiliar with its ways, we naturally yielded ourselves to a process of instruction and gracious integration. A real experience this was—participating in the formalities and amenities of the early-twentieth-century missionary household. The Mattoxes had resided in China over twenty-five years. Standards and customs of domestic life had been adopted from the British missionary community, which had largely set the original patterns for foreign residents in Hangchow. Thus, Chinese courtesy and English formalism pretty well agreed in according Dr. Mattox, as senior Presbyterian resident and chief of the college staff, a social status of special honor and dignity. We found ourselves quite amazed at the impressive corps of servants: At the head ranked the household manager and head of the kitchen; next came the house boy, who served meals and attended to general ordering up and cleanliness; the amah was number three, a woman doing bedroom work, laundry, and mending (no children to care for here); the fourth servant was rated as outdoor coolie, charged with attending to lawn and garden, running errands, and occasional ricksha-pulling. How interesting it was to learn that the root meaning of *ku-lee* is "bitter strength."

Considerable ingenuity was required, with plenty of gesticulation, to make our needs known when the host was absent. Readily we fell into the relaxing habit of afternoon tea, the hour for dinner being seven thirty. Food proved to be of high quality, prepared mostly in Western style, and measuring up to the urgencies of our post–sea voyage appetites, while the once-a-week Chinese meal speedily became an event to look forward to. The roomy house with many windows and double verandas, all screened in, adapted to semitropical climate and open-air living, provided a comfortable abode and offered a ranging vision of ceaseless delight.

Ordinarily the first task of the missionary is to study the language. In our case this was to be deferred due to extreme shortage of teaching staff, the Mission authorities thus assigning us to a preliminary year of teaching. At the same time we learned of the appealing prospect of having the following year at the North China Union Language School in Peking, a privilege for which we would hardly have dared to dream. For teaching work, the Pekingese Mandarin was rated more scholarly and universal, as compared with local dialects; and in a rather popularized form, it was already tending to become the accepted mode of speech for educational purposes throughout China. The Hangchow dialect, though originally a localized Mandarin, had many different sounds and colloquial idioms, as we were to learn later. The written characters, of course, prevailed identical throughout the whole of China.

Monday morning brought the opportunity to plunge directly into the academic program. It seemed good to be on the job, and the students, all boys, showed an equal eagerness. At the moment of my stepping into the classroom, all rose to their feet to greet the new teacher. Such courtesy, never accorded in any of my previous teaching experience, came as a heartwarming surprise. Later it became clear that this gracious custom expressed the traditional respect offered the teacher in a society where learning had long been revered and the privilege available to only a few. Immediately we sensed the students' eagerness and diligence in studies, which would make teaching a constant pleasure and discipline seldom a problem.

One aspect of the classroom, quite new and at first disconcerting, was the unrelieved uniformity of all black hair. For a while this tended to carry a deceptive sense of facial uniformity as well. Actually the shades of complexion and feature types differed widely, including quite white skins and narrowly arched noses. Fortunately, the custom of wearing black, high-buttoned student uniforms, common in Japanese and Chinese government schools, was not in vogue here. A variety of gowns relieved the otherwise severe formality and helped to give expression to the innate individualism of students.

Obviously the days of braided pigtails were past. They had been left behind a decade earlier, when the Manchu dynasty, which had imposed the custom, was overthrown and the Chinese Republic established. Not only had traditional skullcaps been abandoned generally and modern-style haircuts been introduced, but one could detect an alertness to every new mode from America. Presently we noted several of the boys wearing, instead of the smooth hair style, a distinct curl. One of them curiously inquired of the new Lady Teacher, did she do the curling of Mr. Lau's hair? Seemingly, in one respect at least, I was on the way to acceptance as a popular idol.

Just how successfully could one communicate through the English language, with Chinese being the prevailing tongue all around? The effectiveness of our teaching appeared to hinge upon this issue. While a disturbing thought, it proved not an insurmountable problem. Actually, there was no fumbling in the plans. The first requirement of a new missionary is to step firmly into the path of need. In the English language department the special need had arisen because two of its members were on furlough. So it turned out that the major portion of instruction by each of us was English reading and composition. I also carried courses in European history, economics, and current events, while the Lady added sociology. Bible courses, required of all, had been fully provided for; but political science, in which we both had specialized, was not yet introduced.

The demand for English was something astounding. It was also surprising how much of it was taught in senior middle schools, though only the mission schools provided real quality. In the case of the college student, for effective pursuit of modern education, translations of Western studies remained still too limited. Thus a working knowledge of English had become a recognized necessity for the progressive scholar. Besides, it provided the key to the magic door for advanced study abroad, a haunting dream of many a Chinese student.

We were not long discovering that composition classes

laid a heavy burden upon the conscientious teacher. Unless one has attempted the linguistic feat of rearranging Chinese idiomatic expressions into acceptable English grammatical forms, he has missed one of the major tests of ingenuity and patience. Attending rewards were not entirely lacking, as unsuspected flashes of meaning were bound to break through odd forms of construction and word use. A classic example was that of a student who, after absence for Chinese New Year, appeared in new gown, and inquired of Mrs. Lau, "Do you realize me?" While the art of the "singing commercial" may well have been invented in ancient China, the current English-language advertisements were also carrying their peck of spice. The eager egg merchant's handbill declared, "Each egg is carefully examined and tasted to ensure fresh," and the tailor shop's attractively read, "Nice ladies can have fits here."

Only a few days sufficed for us to feel ourselves identified with Hangchow Christian College. This was an institution of approximately one hundred students in the upper level and one hundred and twenty in the preparatory academy, with total teaching and administrative staff adding up to thirty, of which two thirds were Chinese.

In our semitropical climate, the autumn months were declared to be the finest of the year; however, a little convincing seemed called for during the first three days of gloom and drizzle. That shoes could develop mold overnight and underwear feel soggy in the morning unless tucked into bed came as a surprising discovery. Finally, on our fourth day, the September sun broke through in glory, opening up a marvelous vista in every direction. Then we began to realize what a happy lot had fallen to us in having been called to share one of the choice college campus settings in the world.

Chinese romanticism had long before supplied the imaginative name of Dragon Hills. From the main mountain ridge three branches extended down to the river, each being regarded as the head of a mythical dragon dipping down into the water. The three bluffs had for ages been preserved as propitious burial grounds for distinguished families and had been thickly dotted with tombs.

A survey of surrounding valleys brought the assurance of rich harvests of rice and beans, with mulberry groves bespeaking an area of silk culture, and the terraced hillsides displaying their wealth of tea gardens. The broad river offered abundant catches for the fishermen's nets, and upon its surface boats of commerce sailed by the score. Seldom could one find a more idyllic sight than that "fleet of white butterflies" riding the silvery waters, as it was carried by the tide around the great bend. Then, far outward rose the mountain peaks, seeming to flash their warning signals of the approach to the rapids in the gorges.

Towering at the eastern edge of the campus, close beside the river, stood the majestic thirteen-story landmark, Hangchow's famous Six Harmony Pagoda. In the distance, the range of the eye could catch two close-in mountaintops bearing temple roofs, orange walls, camphor trees, and bamboo groves. Secluded in the valleys, still awaiting our visits, nestled a series of Buddhist monasteries in their peaceful retreat.

The treacherous tidal wave (one of the very few tidal bores of the world) rolling in from the Hangchow Bay had done much to determine the character of the city. Instead of an atmosphere of commercial developments and ocean-going trade, the predominant aura had traditionally become one of relative seclusion and of riches in culture. In poetic language, the city with its romantic West Lake and charming environs had long been known as "Heaven Below," signifying its aesthetic, cultural, and spiritual attractions.

We could not help feeling that all this wealth of natural endowment and historical achievement awaited our exploring. The golden autumn months to mid-December lured us out on Saturday hikes and tours. Familiar to us became the sights and sounds and smells of our new country: the ancient footpaths, which the rich and infirm traversed by sedan chair; the artistic temple courts fragrant with incense; the long lines of pilgrims paying annual visits to the shrines; and the refreshing cup of steaming tea graciously offered in a monastery. Then there were the hardy groups of peasants flailing the rice, grass cutters shaving the hillsides for fuel, village women beating their laundry by the stream, carriers chanting to the swing of their load, and fishing boats huddled while casting their nets. Familiar also were the fairy lanes winding through bamboo groves and lofty mountain peaks opening their vistas far and wide.

What about Hangchow proper as capital of the province? Here resided a teeming population estimated at eight hundred thousand, with thriving business enterprises connected to Shanghai by rail and to interior towns by river and canal transport. Busy and somewhat isolated as we were on our suburban campus, only gradually did we make acquaintance of the Inner City.

The three Presbyterian compounds were located in different sections, one belonging to the Presbyterian Church U.S. For over sixty years our Mission (Presbyterian Church U.S.A.) had been operating there, our total staff at this time being twenty, with services covering a range of city and country evangelism, the major share of Christian educational work, and a helping hand in the British Mission Hospital.

Among other leading mission groups, the Church Missionary Society (Anglican) was the strongest, this especially being due to its noted C. M. S. Hospital with extensive clinical services and a training school. Vigorous work was carried on by American Baptists, by China Inland Mission, and also the Y.M.C.A. under missionary direction. Actually, the position of seniority was held by the French Catholics (Lazarist) whose mission had a church reputed to be three hundred years old.

Thus, the series of mission compounds stood as strong centers of influence and service on behalf of the gospel of Christ, as they met pressing social and spiritual needs. A "compound" was a group of buildings enclosed within walls, and this had been the universal arrangement in China for both dwellings and institutions. The college campus, located out in the country and planned on a daring new principle, presented an outstanding exception by its complete openness.

The total missionary personnel in Hangchow, including the college staff, probably stood at over fifty, making a sizable gathering at the monthly Missionary Association meetings. We found these periodic group contacts expressive of the spirit of cooperation and general unity of purpose. Indeed, most areas and phases of work were well laid out so as not to be competitive, but rather complementary. Such occasional evenings of social and cultural intercourse offered refreshing diversion and broadening experience. Usually we managed to participate in the monthly English-language Union Vesper Service, conducted in the hospital chapel. Anything other than such interdenominational spirit would have countered our cherished ideal of united fellowship and witness.

While the richly endowed and progressive province of Chekiang, with population of over twenty million, had begun to establish a few specialized schools for nursing and educational training, Hangchow Christian College stood unique in its program and position of higher education. It alone provided full training for academic degrees of Bachelor of Arts and Bachelor of Science.

How could one help wondering what early visions, infant beginnings, and prayerful efforts lay behind our elaborate layout so imposingly set upon the historic Dragon Hills? Eagerly we gathered the threads of an inspiring story—the beginnings of Christian education and the makings of a Christian college. Protestant missions, at this time, had already developed thirteen Christian colleges and universities, distributed throughout China.

To the venerable D. B. McCartee, M.D., pioneer missionary in Ningpo, 1845, falls the credit of being founder of this institution of Christian learning. Also, the honor of having opened at Ningpo the first permanent Presbyterian mission station in China rests with him. Consonant with the Calvinist tradition, he immediately saw the necessity of training leadership for the developing Chinese church and opened a boarding school with a couple of boys. According to the records, after fifteen years the school had an enrollment of eighteen boys, seven of whom were committed Christians, five from believing families. Evangelism and education clung hand to hand. General literary knowledge, music, and Bible formed the indispensables for preparing ministers and teachers. Through a self-help system, the boys worked at trades, receiving free all food, lodging, clothing, medicine, and teaching. Since some of the boys were indentured to the school for six years, out of this practice arose the uncomplimentary term "Rice Christians."

Apparently the fruits of this budding educational venture soon began to show in the quality of its graduates. Among the early pioneer preachers remembered for their distinguished ministry in the area was the revered Pastor Pao Kuang-hsi, from whose family have since proceeded several generations of devoted ministers. Equally cherished is Pastor Tsang Nying-kwe, who, having first served as teacher and catechist in Ningpo, gave a leading hand in opening the Presbyterian Mission in Hangchow. By him was founded in 1866 the original Protestant church in this city, with which connection stands a legacy of rich and memorable ministry.

In time arose the vision of transferring the thriving Ningpo Boys' School to the heart of Chekiang Province. Hangchow would naturally offer a base geographically more central and strategically more attractive. By sharing its workers, the Ningpo station had already extended its range to "opening Hangchow," and by the following year, 1867, the transfer of the school was realized. Within the advantageous setting of the chief city, new opportunities loomed and a superior status was about to be gained. Soon the Hangchow Presbyterian Boys' School became widely known as the fountain from which trained leadership kept steadily flowing for the needs of the church in the newly awakened society.

Under the direction of Samuel Dodd and with the assistance of John L. Nevius (from Ningpo) the academic offerings of the school increased to include science, philosophy, and theology. In this flourishing condition, and with broader training, it would be just a step to attain the status of a college. After Dr. and Mrs. J. H. Judson arrived in 1880, courses covered the complete high school curriculum and enrollment moved up to thirty-four. The size again doubled by 1893, when Dr. and Mrs. Mattox came to assist in plans calling for reorganization and expansion, with five years of middle school and five years of college. Thus, by 1905, fifty years after the school's birth, about six hundred students had been in attendance. Of the eighty-two graduates there were twenty-nine ministers, twenty-four teachers, and twenty-nine pursuing other professional and business interests. The intervening decade had brought forth amazing progress, despite severe cholera epidemics and the massive student riots in the North connected with the "Boxer Uprising," which carried a wave of hatred against foreigners and the Chinese Christians. Officially designated as Hangchow Presbyterian College in 1907 and riding on the crest of the post-Boxer education reform, the school was greatly enriched in curriculum, and the staff was strengthened in both Chinese and missionary personnel. Enrollment reached eighty on the preparatory level and thirty-five in the college.

This, then, was the right time to look forward to a new campus, and within five years the expansive layout of new buildings was constructed on the Dragon Hills, much credit being due to Dr. Robert F. Fitch. To Dr. Judson, who already had devoted thirty years toward realizing his educational dream, was awarded the office of president. Furthermore, the institution was strengthened as it became a joint project of both Presbyterian denominations (Presbyterian Church U.S. and Presbyterian Church U.S.A.).

To me it appealed as a matter of special interest that the completion of major buildings and the opening on the grand site took place in the year of the Republican Revolution, 1911. Our arrival on the scene had come just one decade too late to share in the flush of national rebirth and to witness Dr. Sun Yat-sen's official visit to the campus in the autumn of 1912.

With ample accommodations provided, the new design

called for a "strong college of four hundred students," all college grade. Now considerable attention, with deep searchings and disputations, had to be given to the adequate clarification of the purpose of higher education as a Mission enterprise. To encompass the apparent needs on the field and obtain the cooperation of supporting churches in America, the Board of Directors was led to the formulation of this standing statement:

> The avowed aim of the College is to give a higher education under distinctly Christian auspices and influences to as large a number as possible of Chinese young men with a view of raising up men for leadership in service to the Church, state and human society.

Practically all fields, at this turn of China's history, stood in need of trained leadership, but especially the Christian institutions. For example, the province had many organized places of worship and numerous schools, both primary and middle, under management of the missions.

What opportunity for direct evangelism did we find within the schools? Obviously, our college community offered a ready-made situation; at least 80 percent of the freshmen were coming from non-Christian homes. Basic courses in Bible were naturally required of all, and also attendance at daily chapel services and Sunday worship. Frequently student preaching bands went out to small villages on Sunday afternoons, giving their personal witness. As a rule, once a year a series of special meetings was conducted by an outside evangelist, whose dramatic instruction and fervent appeal heightened the spiritual tone and brought forth decisions of commitment to Christ. Shortly prior to our coming, the college church had experienced a pentecostal occasion of record inflow: forty-nine students publicly confessed Christ and twenty-three received baptism.

Some of our students we found deeply in earnest about their faith and its promise for the ills of society. One of them, from a Hangchow Christian family, unburdened his heart to me thus: "Turn to my country, and what a miserable sight I see! The government is in the worst corruption, the people are in ignorance and poverty. Bandits rise here and there. Is there nothing I can do for it? As a young man of China, my responsibility is heavy. I shall try to deliver our people out of ignorance and teach them to be right and true. I shall try to bring them to Jesus Christ, for he can save them and my country out of sin and darkness to a better and happier condition." (After graduation, David Chen joined the staff of the local Y.M.C.A. and shortly thereafter suffered a fatal illness.)

"God forbid that we make education an end in itself," proclaimed Dr. James R. Yen, the rising young leader of the mass education movement. By his project of holding night classes for adults, using his one thousand selected characters, he was aiming to open up to the masses the printed "Word." This passion for overcoming illiteracy lay rooted in his Christian faith: "By the grace of God," he said, "we must capture China for Christ."

But it was appropriate to ask, Are these formal means of Biblical instruction and "pressure" evangelism by themselves adequate expressions of the gospel? It was certainly not so regarded. Other means and influences, less vocal, were consistently and pervasively at work. The spirit and manner of wholesome and kindly daily living, keen interest in the personal welfare and mental development of others, stress upon honesty in studies and habits of integrity, the example of a teaching job well done—these, rather than intellectual exercise or emotional impulse, were felt to be the basic elements of Christian witness and the patterns of Christian life. In many respects our mission and message had the character of being quietly implied rather than blatantly declared. Perhaps this was particularly appropriate to the Chinese mind and mood; mass conversions were extremely uncommon.

2

FIRST YEAR IN CHINA

CHINA'S OPENNESS to Western influences in the early twenties brought in a flood of workers and visitors. Our coming was part of the wave of Protestant missionaries, which then had reached the high peak of over five thousand. Also, various interested specialists were visiting leading centers to lecture by invitation. Jane Addams, pioneer in social work at the Chicago Hull House, conducted conferences at the Hangchow Y.W.C.A. Professor John Dewey, of Columbia University, moved among academic circles, broadcasting ideas on the empirical method in education. Bertrand Russell unloaded Oxford University philosophical wisdom in the land of ancient sages. Returning home, he wrote a book entitled *The Problem of China*, without venturing to offer any solutions. In it he frankly confessed, "When I went to China, I went to teach, but every day I stayed I thought less of what I had to teach them and more of what I had to learn from them." The third of the "wise men" who came offering their gifts was Sherwood Eddy. To educational method and philosophical insight he added spiritual experience. International Y.M.C.A. secretary and noted world traveler, he toured China, speaking to vast crowds of students with the power of an impassioned evangelist. In dramatic fashion he laid out China's ills and problems, proclaiming that there was no hope of solution apart from the transforming power of Jesus Christ. These appeals to the hungers and aspirations of youth brought remarkable response.

China has long been regarded as somewhat enigmatic. Yet, here we were face to face, though in a limited area, with the things that make the land and people at once mysterious and engaging. How can one describe an elaborate sunset or put into words the complexities of a national exhibit? Equally, how can one sketch the multitude of experiences and impressions that flood a first year in China? Objects of beauty, fascinating customs, endearing friendships—all these accumulate, and to them are added the trials of the flesh and spirit.

It is all too common to carry into the ancient Orient a critical and superior mood, contrasting "backward" conditions with our "progressive" ways of the West. The sense of our spiritual call could not outweigh the fact of being guests in China. Perhaps the first expressions of love are appreciation and identification. Though we ourselves were lacking in the Chinese social disciplines of patience and reasonableness, of wisdom and courtesy, we soon were awarded the gratifying feeling of being accepted. Anyway, far from looking backward, the temper of the student was to thirst for the latest thing.

Among the pleasures of teaching were our practical field trips. Sociology and economics classes joined to visit the provincial prison, the national mint, match and silk factories—all in Hangchow. Instead of teacher conducting students, it would be more accurate to say that they took us. Certainly, ours was a learning together. Also, by small groups we mingled with farmers in the rice paddies and visited outlying villages, observing local handicraft, primary schools, and conditions of common domestic life.

Fortunately, our campus managed to avoid student strikes. Thus we missed some of the excitement we might have found in our experience of college life. Strikes, an idea borrowed from labor practice in the West, were sprouting up widely as a current malady in the institutions of higher education. Apparently the new concept of democracy and self-government was proving to be heady stuff. The demands might be for dismissing an unacceptable teacher or relaxing some disciplinary rule. At other times student demonstrations had the object of awakening public opinion to the failures of governmental policies. Our Mission colleges tended to look with tolerance upon such academic interruptions, regarding them as newfound means of expression and as a phase of learning that freedom without responsibility spells chaos.

Impressively, nature's gifts stood lavish on the Dragon Hills. Their glory, varying with the seasons, brought unexpected delight and fascination. Most of the hillsides round about were annually subjected to a clean clipping to provide household fuel; often even roots were not spared. Our preserve, however, after ten years of conservation, had grown into a paradise of trees, shrubs, and wild flowers, affording sanctuary for wild animals and varieties of birds. We became accustomed to the bark of the deer, the whirr of the pheasant, the call of the cuckoo, and the graceful sweep of the paradise flycatcher. But we also had warning of the deadly cobra, which was dangerous when disturbed on a dark path at night. The caution: Never fail to carry a light.

Each season, in turn, kept presenting its own charms. Autumn announced its arrival with splashes of crimson on the candleberry tree, as if to melt away the wax from the white-coated seed clusters. Winter, with its fleeting gifts of fluffy blankets of snow, held the ample adornments of ruby-red berries on bushes of wild holly and the heavenly bamboo. Surprisingly early and rich came the spring, spreading the entire hillsides with an amazing profusion of pink azaleas, to be followed by clumps of lavender rhododendrons overhanging rock and crag.

May had pleasantly set for us a little private natural experiment. The houseboy surprised us with a gift of three hundred silkworms, little wiggly things just hatched from tiny eggs the size of a pinhead. The Hangchow silks were known to have been prized by the Imperial families from ancient times, when their royal barges carried the precious cargo of silks and rice up the Grand Canal. Now it became our privilege to observe nature's mysterious process in silk culture. I doubt that anyone in America ever undertook to mother so large a family of pets.

Several weeks of nursing our ravenous brood with quantities of luscious mulberry leaves produced a horde of plump inch-and-a-half-long worms. Suddenly all appeared sick or on a hunger strike for a few days, with the resulting marvel of shedding their old gray skins. Coming out fresh and firm, appetite restored, they soon were ready to spin their silvery cocoons, entombing themselves in shrouds of pure silk. Usually, for the comfort and vanities of man, a wholesale sacrifice is demanded of these creatures. Instead of completing the cycle and being transfigured into the moth that lays the egg, the pupa has to lose its life. Otherwise, by eating its way out of the cocoon, the pupa cuts the silk, so that it cannot be unraveled as a thread. The industrial process, in this case, is by steam-killing. But we, out of mercy and curiosity, observed the emergence of a few lovely moths.

To be guests in China means many things, especially that of sharing the joys of their elaborate festivals. At such times all hearts are open in generosity and gaiety. The outstanding feast is China New Year, so called because it follows the traditional calendar. Coming late in January and extending two weeks or more, it constitutes a total festivity, including the social elements of our customary Christmas, New Year, and Easter combined. Not observing any Sunday, except as practiced by Christian communities, this one time of the year everyone was enjoying an extended holiday. For several days all business closed shop, families having already made ample provision for abundance of food and acquired a new stock of clothing. Everywhere streets and homes are gaudy with banners and lanterns of festal red, best garments are displayed, greetings are extended and gifts exchanged. For a fortnight the tensions of life seem to be forgotten; standing accounts have been somehow cleared for a new start, a relaxed mood takes over and the spirit is one of renewal and hope.

Our college calendar was so arranged that students went home for a long "midsemester." Chinese friends came to our house to bring greetings and invite us to join their families for New Year delicacies. One of the special dishes for the occasion, which we directly adopted as a favorite, is glutinous rice with honeyed dates. By custom, this was neatly wrapped in cornhusk and served from a steaming kettle. These times of relaxing offered warmth and insight.

Wherever the church is there is Christmas. Yet our first yuletide in China had to be acknowledged as a somewhat drab and fleeting event. Not only no family gathering but practically no holiday made it a different experience. Classes were dismissed for one day only in order to lengthen the winter vacation. Nevertheless, in churches, including our chapel, the birth of the Christ-child was joyfully celebrated. In fervor, the message of the incarnation was preached and taught and dramatized. All seemed natural enough when we mingled with the students putting up decorations and preparing the pageantry, and when the adorable little children played their part in the program. The final event, hailed by hearty cheering, was the arrival of Father Christmas, followed by two attendants carrying huge baskets. From these he distributed a little pack of candy and nuts for each person present. Then, at midnight, we heard a joyful caroling from house to house over the campus.

High among our social events stood the notable wedding. How fortunate to be able to count within the experiences of our first year one of the finest of Christian weddings. Two highly esteemed families, clans of the Changs and Wangs, of two noted cities, gathered to have son and daughter united in holy wedlock. This union would embody the traditional significance of favorable parental and environmental background, making it both propitious and romantic. The groom would bring the noble qualities of the Hangchow man and the bride bear the feminine traits of virtue and beauty accorded to the Soochow woman. Sinpei Chang held the heritage of staunch Presbyterian parents; his grandfather was a minister and his father a well-established Hangchow physician. Dorothy Yang was the daughter of a leading Methodist clergyman in Soochow, where also the Methodist hospital and university work were centered.

This pair was an ideal example of an attractive and modernized couple. Both had been studying in America, he qualifying medically as eye, ear, and nose specialist and she being trained as a nurse. The setting and ceremony of this wedding were apparently designed as a blending of the customs of East and West. In true Chinese form, the bride was brought in the old-style bridal chair to the groom's home, and the later festivities all took place there. But the vows were taken in the church at the altar, Dr. Mattox officiating. The entire ceremony followed the latest American customs, including wedding march, bridesmaids, groom's attendants, flower girls and all. Western-style dress was adopted, the bride wearing a lovely white train and veil, while the groom had long-tailed black coat, silk hat, and white spats. These completely non-Chinese aspects, we were told, represented a concession to the promptings of their modernistic friends, all returned students. (This "new breed" consisted of leaders in public administration and professional life, including our college dean, Andrew Wu, just returned with higher degrees from Princeton.) Even to us, so new from the West, such a parade of foreign styles seemed quite incongruous with the native setting; to most of the Chinese it must have presented a strangely disturbing sight.

Almost immediately after the ceremony, to our surprise, the retreating couple was heavily showered with handfuls of rice, an act signifying good wishes for prosperity and fruitfulness. Then, the reception in the ancestral home of the Chang family brought us into a truly Chinese environment. Entering a spacious hall, richly draped with silk hangings and bordered by red-and-gold scrolls, we faced the semicircle of the bridal party. And what a transformation! Before us stood the bride and her maids exquisitely garbed, Chinese-style, in Hangchow brocade silk of crimson and gold, the colors symbolic of happiness and abundance. Feasting was in order; and not unlike at the marriage of Cana, wine had a place in ceremony and merriment. Before departing, we were even privileged a peep into the room for the newlyweds—the lovely silk-laden bedchamber prepared for a princess and her lord.

A missionary to a far land does not willingly magnify the problems of his physical and social adjustments. He has come to live, to learn, and to share. Yet it should be frankly acknowledged that our year of apprenticeship carried its weight of burdens and strains. From the first we found the language barrier a limiting and frustrating experience. Our lack of free communication occasioned many inconveniences and mutual misunderstandings. Only the kind assistance and unfailing forbearance of others carried us through the daily affairs, while often we suffered a stupefying sense of being shut out from the surrounding world of thought.

The semitropical climate, to our surprise, proved rather difficult, especially for Grace. On the whole we felt the autumn months to be bright and stimulating. So also, March came along early with its balmy sweetness. But the penetrating cold of January–February brought its touch of bitterness, and the sultry atmosphere of May–June proved withering and debilitating. In that temperate latitude of thirty-two degrees, the high humidity caused much discomfort.

It was not the custom to have heating provisions (other than sunshine) for winter, and all buildings of school and church were cheerless. To Chinese teachers and students this was a familiar situation, to be met by bundling up in long padded garments (some fur-lined) with extending sleeves serving as muffs. For office work, relief could be provided by setting up a large brazier of glowing charcoal —a blessing to numb fingers. The elderly folk while sitting in church commonly had with them tiny brass braziers, cozily snuggled at their feet. The convenience of rubber hot-water bottles had not yet come into vogue, but the Chinese had long used flat brass bottles for bed-heating.

This effective means of all-night comfort we quickly appropriated.

Fortunately, as newcomers, we had brought a supply of woolen underwear, over which we piled layer after layer of clothing, topped with a burdensome overcoat. To complete the outfit, the local cobbler made up sizable felt shoes, and our hostess knitted half-finger mitts. In spite of all this, the penetrating cold inflicted its miseries, causing us to marvel how uncomplainingly our Chinese fellows suffered these hardships. And what a blessed retreat we still had! Always our foreign-style residential home awaited us with the modest comfort of glowing fireplace or tiny coal-burning stove.

Turning to the other side of the coin, we had to contend with the swelter of tropical heat, and for this we came unprepared. Since the shift of temperature came suddenly, a colleague came to my rescue, offering two spare linen suits —until mine could be tailored. Clear days called for the protection of cork-filled sun helmets and, for foot-ease, lightweight canvas shoes. Less simple than adapting to the blazing sun was the encounter with those muggy and stifling days which left us listless and languid. And what a battle with the thriving crop of mold! Shoes, hatband, briefcase, and books called for constant wiping, as did the greenish-yellow blotches that appeared by magic on the plastered walls of our room.

Surprisingly enough, we had the convenience of electricity. It was supplied from the city plant by special line, to be used for lighting only, and required strict conservation. (Anyway, our forethought in bringing a kerosene lamp was to be rewarded on later occasions.) But as to fans and refrigerators, these remained unknown luxuries. We depended, as the Chinese had for ages, on the graceful maneuvering of the ever-present hand fan. Another cooling device, rarely used, although I recall an occasion or so, was an Indian punkah in perpetual motion over the dinner table—with the rope and tugging hand effectively concealed.

I doubt that any amount of warning could have made us fully aware of the problems of sanitation. Hygienic standards and practices common in the West had scarcely ranged beyond the hospital walls. How could one safeguard against the lurking perils of infection and contagion? As to food and drink, the only safe rule was to take it hot. Everything required cooking, except nuts in shell, while raw fruit needed to be steeped before peeling. Other health advice ran like this: Never walk anywhere in bare feet; give hands a frequent soap cleansing; discipline fingers never to touch the eyes—lest they carry the dread trachoma; bring your barber into the house where you can be assured of sterilized tools; battle with unfailing vigilance against the malaria-spreading mosquito. All these matters had to become habitual.

Another example of adaptation, a bit awkward to begin with, pertained to our toilet situation. Fortunately, we enjoyed the benefit of running cold water (in rainy seasons), with improvised equipment of enamel washbasin and glamorous tin tub. Instead of flush toilet, available accommodations consisted simply of a commode containing a tall, porcelain chamber jar—which hardly appeared totally adequate! After my fruitless search for the additional outhouse, I was advised that all could be taken care of properly inside. This implied the aid of plenty of disinfecting fluid and timely disposal by servants.

Social problems presented their challenge. Many of them, quite at variance with our familiar patterns, tended to arouse our sympathies and offend our ethical sense.

These called for analysis and understanding. The ricksha, as a mode of transportation, we accepted without much question, chiefly because it offered about the only way of getting around. Except for the matter of conserving our own time and energy, we would rather have walked, as we often did.

Ricksha-pulling was reckoned as a worthy public service, not demeaning, though a burdensome and exhausting form of labor. Pulling another person on wheels or carrying by sedan chair was not unlike the business of a farmer growing food for society. For both it is a means of livelihood that taxes human strength, because no easier ways have been thus far provided. One could respect and admire the ricksha puller for his pride in strength, speed, and endurance, and for the pleasure he took in bargaining for the fare. Yet as a matter of personal ethics I could not escape the sense of degradation. Perhaps it was I who was degraded by accepting shelter and ease from a fellowman who by exposure and strain shortened his life on my behalf. Of course there were other more serious forms of drudgery, gravely inhuman, but of less direct personal implication. There was the sight of the human teams dragging unmercifully heavy cartloads of rice over the arched bridge on the Shanghai Bund, and the towing of loaded cargo boats against the swift rapids of the Yangtze Gorges.

Most distressing was the prevalence of beggars. If one's heartstrings were tugged at the thought of their misery, the mind likewise was repulsed at the sight of their degradation. Fortunately they never appeared on the campus as it was too far out of town and known to be forbidden. But just enter the city and they came running imploringly. Throw a coin to one and a dozen popped up, small children being pushed to the fore. These were mostly professionals,

horribly filthy and making begging their trade. We found
the best practical answer was to try to ignore them, which
seemed totally hardhearted. People who are honorably
destitute through misfortune, we were told, usually find
family and friends to help them.

Beggar gangs, as a rule, were organized under a leader
and kept moving from town to town. Local authorities
made no attempt to deal with the problem except paying
them off so that they would leave for a while. The pilgrim
season, when thousands came from distant areas to worship at the famous temples and monasteries, was always
heyday for beggars. They lined the paths, exposing their
horrible wounds (often sham), crying out, "Do merit, do
merit." In this way a good harvest was assured from the
devout worshipers. As for ourselves, in the manner of the
priest and the Levite in Biblical writ, we "passed by on the
other side." Here was a dreadful social malady, a challenge
to enlightened government and to the church, awaiting a
"New Order" of constructive planning and rehabilitation.

An alarming situation was presented by reports of ban-
ditry—an obvious symptom of unstable government. The
night attack on a train (Peking "Express") in a northern
province stirred quite an international commotion, as it involved a group of foreigners being kidnapped for ransom.
Quickly we wrote to our families that our area remained
peaceful and safe. Actually, the Central Government was
ready to crumble; and local areas, in spite of elected assemblies, were lapsing into the hands of warlords using merce-
nary troops. These soldiers, very poorly paid, and having
no concern for the local people, readily turned to pillage
and violence. Entire families were killed and suffering was
widespread. And it all came close to us when a student of
our province told of his own village's being plundered and
the family home burned down.

Now our initial year of missionary life had come to its close. What did it speak to us, out of the vast flood of new experiences? Before us stood the significant fact: that beyond our little community of youth and aspiration, of idealism and learning, so fittingly set upon the grand Dragon Hills, lay a land of many troubles and a people of great need. Faced with these social ills and spiritual hungers, it stood as our mission: to learn, to teach, to share, to hope, and to pray that from the knowledge and fruits of Christian faith and practice China might come to envision and attain her new day.

3

AMONG THE MANDARINS

*A*FTER THE SWELTERING DAYS of the semester's final exams, the general exodus at the end of June left the campus hushed and forsaken. Families, with children, hurried off to Mokanshan, nearby summer resort, for the mountain's refreshing breezes and invigorating night air. Our compass directed us farther north, several hundred miles up the coast by steamship. We had planned a rendezvous with Stanton and Sarah—our first chance to get together in China. They were still stationed in Chefoo, a thriving port on the north side of the Shantung Peninsula, and this would be right on our way as we proceeded to Peking for the coming year's language study.

In Hangchow there remained a little unfinished business before we could leave our locale, abounding with treasures uniquely its own. We wanted to express our greetings and impress our families with the nature and quality of Hangchow products. The Christmas season had come around too soon; besides, we had quickly learned that the missionary salary was geared only to bare necessities.

Select items in the homebound packages included samples of the famous Dragon Well tea, long ranking as the favorite of Imperial families; hand-painted West Lake folding fans from the "world's largest" fan shop, boasting its one hundred varieties; ornamental articles made of the choicest native silk from the noted Great Street Silk Store; and also quaint hand-fashioned steel scissors of various styles and sizes. Thus, in the tradition of Marco Polo, who seven centuries before our time had astonished Europe with tales and objects from the "noble city of Quinsay," we felt the urge to spread the fame of present-day Hangchow.

Our summer interlude in Chefoo with my brother and his jolly mate fulfilled all expectations. Practically for the first time since our youthful days on the Canadian farm was such an occasion of leisure provided for gadding around together and sharing viewpoints. There were donkey rides and picnics as we spied out the area, observing local customs and mission activities, while many an evening became a wanton sacrifice to hilarious rounds of Pit. It came to Grace and me that, by years of tightly scheduled programs, we had practically lost the spirit of play, whereas our hosts had happily managed to retain the lighter side of life.

The impression remains of being surprised and somewhat shocked at the superior missionary housing: substantial stone structures with rather elegant interiors. These, compared with our Hangchow Mission property, seemed to bespeak the solid and conservative character of the North. Chefoo could claim the honor of being the earliest Mission station in the so-called Sacred Province, home of the revered Confucius. As early as 1861 the noted Hunter Corbett and John L. Nevius began evangelistic and educational activities from this base, leaving a heritage of vigorous church life and strong medical work. Also there was in operation a well-patronized Christian Business School (Yih Wen), well adapted to a port of considerable commerce. Stanton and Sarah, while still drumming at the language (though already speaking it glibly) toward proficiency in communication, also were filling important posts in this school. Such needful ministries of medical care and business training provided doors through which many, young and old, were brought to the knowledge of Jesus Christ.

September 22, 1923, marked our arrival in Peking, exactly one year from the date of first landing in Shanghai. Ah, such a voyage as we had experienced from Chefoo to Tientsin! The wiles of the China Sea in typhoon season lend praise to the worthy decorum of the vast Pacific. As we embarked on the coastal steamer late in the afternoon, typhoon signals gave warning of a rough passage ahead. Perhaps this explains why there was on board only one first-class passenger besides us; others taking the trip were settled in steerage.

Scarcely fifteen minutes had passed of the twenty-four-hour voyage before we became terribly seasick and helpless; forthwith we cast ourselves into our bunks without thought of shedding boots or garments. Everything not fully secured on the ship began shifting and banging, water slashing against the cabin door and our luggage pieces ceaselessly tumbling to and fro. All through the long night we tossed wretchedly, until a slight easement came around six A.M., enabling me to raise up for removal of raincoat and shoes. To our great relief, we then had some sleep, awakening at ten o'clock with the urge to get tidied up and restore our sense of balance.

The hardy British captain later intimated, as we shared the afternoon meal, that this trip would go down in the books as a really tough one. He explained that the larger coastal vessels had all been called over to Japan for emergency service in the aftermath of the terrible Tokyo earthquake. Consequently, our little brig, with scarcely any weighty cargo, was left to take the storm. "I tell you," he confided, "she just about rolled her insides out." At dusk we floated smoothly up the winding river to enter harbor and confront the Westernized port of Tientsin.

Next morning, after repose and refreshment at the Missionary Home, a three-hour train trip delivered us to the Peking railway station, just outside the Chien Men (Front Gate). Along the way, we had noticed that crops and modes of farming differed considerably from the Hangchow area. Instead of rice in irrigated valleys, there was corn and millet on the broad plains. Plowing and harrowing was being done by donkey or small ox in dust-blown fields, whereas in the South the water buffalo served to till the rice paddies. One longed to see a real horse; and a rare sight it had been in the street of Chefoo—a soldier leading such a noble animal, probably the prize of a military commander.

So this was Peking, the city of historic Imperial might and grandeur! Before us stood the main gateway with mammoth arched entrance beneath the great ornamental structure towering to nearly one hundred feet and connecting the enormous city wall fifty feet in height. Here we were about to enter a citadel unique in the world. Since we were expected, the Language School Hostel attendant was at hand; and to him and his waiting rickshas we confidently yielded ourselves and baggage.

To our delight, we found the hostel for housing language students a distinctly Chinese type of dwelling. In earlier days it had been the home of a Manchu prince. Upon entering the narrow gate of the walled enclosure, we viewed a brick-paved courtyard with a prominent hall-like structure. The three sides consisted of a series of connected dwellings, all on one level and with two rooms each. Favored with a choice, as early arrivals, we picked a unit on the sunny side and began to feel at home in a new kind of simplicity. The total establishment proved to consist of three courts, with two main halls for social and dining purposes; but apart from the ornamental construction of the halls with also some appropriate Chinese furnishings, little of the once-princely atmosphere remained. Nevertheless, a great deal of linguistic and cultural study would be required before our group of raw Westerners could play the part. But, directly, the call to lunch achieved the first step in that direction—Chinese food, Pekingese-style, was reported to be on the menu once a week.

We felt pleased with the rather artless aspect of our abode; and, besides, it was delightful to be "just students" again—with the Mission paying our rent and fees. Our little suite presented a freshness of having just been all redone. Golden straw matting covered the floor of gray-stone pavement, walls were modestly tinted and the ceiling pure white. Windows, consisting merely of clear rice paper attached to the latticed frames, had the quality of being luminous without any transparency. And, a centrally located sheet-iron coal stove stood assuringly against the chills of a Northern winter. One discovery waited for a later day and was first made, unsuspectingly, by the next-door resident. He had heard patterings and scratchings overhead at night, as we had also. Being annoyed, he picked up his slipper and shied it upward. What an amazement when it didn't come back! The ceiling, like the windows, turned out to be just plain white paper. Anyway, he really scared the mouse.

Immediately we became aware that our new environment presented sights and sounds totally unknown in the former rustic, ivory-tower surroundings. This was now city life, and along with that a lot of Northern flavor. Each morning we awakened to the call of street vendors; and to our unskilled ears, these melodious tones sounded something like "ha-le-lu-yah"—which probably declared the arrival of some fresh vegetable or breakfast pastry. Birds, though scarcely ever noticeable in the trees (except sparrows), appeared to hold a favored place; but alas, in a state of captivity. A peep outside the court at dawn: there strolled a local shopkeeper carrying his bird. They will not sing, it was said, without this sense of morning freshness and freedom. Yet these feathered songsters were carried in the cage or sometimes openly on a small stick with a slender cord attached to the foot. Pigeons also played their peculiar role, making melody for all the city to hear. What were these delicate tones floating out of the sky, almost daily around ten A.M.? To me it sounded like the singing strains of telephone wires at sub-zero, but actually it was a flock of Peking pigeons making their rounds with tiny flutes attached to their legs, and apparently enjoying their concert as much as we did.

Soon we learned that one of the choice dishes at a feast in the North is Peking duck. However, all evidence indicated that the common, everyday form of protein consisted of plain pork. A chorus of grunts and squeals, within hearing of our hostel, meant that a drove of swine was being herded along Pig Street to supply the hog market nearby. As merchants and butchers took delivery, fantastic sights of transportation met our eyes: half a dozen hogs, legs securely tied, borne along on a huge wheelbarrow, the man struggling at the handles and being aided in balance by a leather band over his shoulders; and again, the rugged two-wheeled Peking cart loaded with twenty squirming pigs, rope network preventing them from rolling off, four men in front strenuously dragging and a fifth pushing and guarding behind. To be sure, compared with our well-rounded porkers in America, these would be rated "scrubby runts."

What also was becoming a familiar sight, though of a very different nature, was the long lines of cargo-bearing camels, with typically Mongolian masters, swinging in from the distant northwest. With these, it soon became natural to associate the biting winter cold and furious dust storms. Unless absolutely necessary, it was sheer folly to attempt facing these fierce blasts of grit and yellow soil. When the Gobi Desert flung forth its golden dust, no building stood proof against its penetration. Our improvised protection, not entirely unavailing, was the setting up of an umbrella over our heads in bed.

Beyond these first elementary impressions of Peking, associated with our arrival and manner of housing and immediate surroundings, lay the fascination of the great Imperial City—ancient in origin, unique in design, and rich in culture. At least a touch of all of this, and perhaps much that ranged beyond the limits of its walls, could be gradually unfolded throughout the year along with our primary objective of language study.

We had come to study Mandarin, the mode of speech long held standard for scholars and officials. It carried prestige and in a somewhat modified form was becoming widely used for schooling. This North China Union Language School (Hwa Yu Hsueh Hsiao), product of enterprising missionary scholars of the North, was designed to provide linguistic knowledge and skill to the incoming flood of foreign personnel—mission, business, and government.

A corps of select Chinese teachers, trained in the technique of direct method, began to portray to us the things of our everyday world by totally new symbols of communication. Instead of being subjected to a dull and labor-some task, we were treated to an exhilarating experience. Each morning, with flashes of imagination and store of good humor, ten new words were introduced to the general group and followed by a series of practice sessions in units of eight, after which the three-hour period came to a close by each of us having a personal drill in a little stall with a private teacher. The afternoon session, being largely rehearsal, meant we had been allowed eight chances to forget—and no more.

Mr. Chang (spoken reversely—Chang Hsien sheng) was the honored and skillful head teacher, while his associate, the youthful, tall, and elegant Mr. Wu soon qualified for the whispered name of Dearest. Presumably, neither spoke or understood any English, their art lying in clear enunciation and graceful, revealing gesture. Not only the meaning had to be made plain, but formation of sound demonstrated by position of mouth and tongue, including muscular operation of the throat.

What might be the first essential words in a totally strange language? Naturally, the primary need for identification calls for the personal pronouns: *wo, ni, ta* ("I," "you," and "he"). Perhaps the next most useful word is "thing." It carries you one step beyond merely pointing at an object and covers an amazingly wide range—inasmuch as "east-west" is the literal Chinese expression for "thing."

That literary methods in the East stand in many ways reversed to ours, we had noticed; books being opened at what we consider the back, and lines of print running vertical instead of horizontal. Now we learned that in modes of speech qualifying adjectives usually take the backward form of following the noun instead of preceding it. The question was, To what length might these various principles operate? One morning one of the words introduced we heard voiced as *tou,* repeated over and over, with gestures indicating it represented some part of the anatomy. Pointing tentatively to different spots, "Chang Teacher" finally reached down to the tip of his foot, whereupon we all nodded with relief that at least one sound corresponded to our native tongue. Then, sharply he shook his head and decisively thumped his finger on his skull. A shock of surprise and a roar of laughter—yes, in the upside-down language of China "the head is the toe" (*tou*).

Our basic language course was designed for two years, one in residence at the school and a second with private tutor in the local area of our work—although for so-called mastery several more years would be needed. A vocabulary of over a thousand words had to be gained the first year, primarily for hearing and speaking and secondarily for reading. To have a complete familiarity with four thousand commonly used characters was reckoned to be fairly proficient in the language. Recognition of these strange symbols, some simple and others extremely complex, presented a challenging test to anyone's mind. And since the language is not phonetic, the structure of the character might give little more than a clue to its meaning; symbol and sound constituted a pair of totally independent acts of memory.

Chinese writing, originating nearly four thousand years ago, naturally began with a series of simple picture markings, called pictographs. Later, this type of communication, highly developed in the hands of scholar and poet, lent itself to brushstrokes of such delicacy and beauty as to produce the notable art of calligraphy.

Character analysis presented an interesting phase of the study, providing scope for ranging imagination. Consider the ingenuity and skill required in creating symbolism to meaningfully represent both concrete objects and abstract ideas. As developed in the early pictographs: In any representation of love a heart sits at the center; forgiveness is a combination of woman, mouth, and heart; the idea of harmony and peace is expressed by a woman under a roof; and for what is right and good, there is a woman with a child at her side.

Much could be said for the advanced methods of language teaching and learning. Little did we realize the toils and frustrations of our earliest missionaries, for instance, the pioneers in Ningpo, 1845. Compared with their dependence upon totally untrained teachers, our facilities and methods at hand ranked splendidly academic. The handsomely red-leather-bound volume of "Mateer" served about as admirably as a cowboy's saddle. Calvin W. Mateer, Presbyterian missionary in Shantung, 1862 to 1908, ranked as evangelist and scholar. Noted as founder of the Tengchow Boys' College and translator of the New Testament into Mandarin, he had also bestowed a precious legacy to future missionaries and other branches of service in China. By his ponderous two-volume work, *Mandarin Language Lessons* in systematically progressive arrangement, the term "Mateer" had come throughout North China to mean Chinese language study.

Equally indispensable and likewise an armload was our inexhaustible "MacGillivary" (British missionary scholar), the 1,200-page *Mandarin-Romanized Dictionary of Chinese*. Every page of it we found richly stacked with character combinations and phrases corresponding to our familiar English expressions.

As an illuminating handbook for understanding and appreciation of the historical development of characters, we enjoyed the aid of the newly published *Analysis of Chinese Characters* by Ingram and Wilder. The original picture form of these symbols and the ingenious building up of component parts for elaborate literary expression was made alive to us by Dr. Ingram's imaginative lectures.

Then there was the flash-card system for character recognition and memory drill. Always our pockets held a pack for the idle minute. Besides, one could feel a real thrill in movements around the city, on discovering street signs or shop fronts bearing distinguishable characters. Similarly, in hearing and speaking practice, what a host of unwary helpers—ricksha pullers, bazaar merchants, temple attendants, and children at play—shared in the training of our faulty ears and bungling tongues.

To conclude that our academic disciplines were confined to language exclusively would be a mistake; they were much broader. Through a series of well-designed weekly lectures, a general orientation opened up the fields of history, geography, society, government, religion, and art. Along with this stimulation, we found the Language School library stocked with many choice books. Also, in the course of observation tours both within and beyond the city this manifold ancient culture kept speaking to us and entering deeply into our experience.

Wisely, I think, the determining of fields and scope of reading was left to individual interest. Only geography required a written test, as a must in basic knowledge. There was no doubt of the need for each to have an elemental grasp of the physical layout of this most culturally unified and most durable civilization. Grover Clark, editor of the *Peking Leader* (American daily), who lectured on history and geography, took us on imagined journeys—even up the perilous Yangtze River Gorges to the western provinces.

An interesting discovery that readily impressed us appeared in many common names of cities and provinces: they were of simple geographical origin. Peking is literally "northern capital" and Shanghai is "up at the sea." So the western province of Szechwan is "four streams" (sources of the two great rivers), and Yunnan Province is "south of the clouds"; similarly our own province of Chekiang is "dominated by the river."

As to the political background, there must have been something tremendously durable about the principles and structure of the Imperial Government. One took note of the theocratic system, wherein the Son of Heaven annually offered a priestly sacrifice on behalf of the whole people upon the great Altar of Heaven. There was the safeguarding principle of royal responsibility in the recognized custom of the emperor's losing his mandate to rule when calamity, through neglect or corruption, overtook the land. And, how durable was the closely knit public administration in the hands of a scholar-based civil service resting upon the examination system! All these elements gave the impression of being worthily founded upon the pillars of wisdom, experience, religion, and learning.

Beyond doubt the most versatile lecturer and electric personality appearing before us was the venerable Arthur H. Smith. This diminutive physical dynamo with remarkable mental agility and rapid-firing tongue had served in China forty years under the American Board (Congregational) Mission and was held in particular esteem for his writings on China. Particularly his two sociological works, *Chinese Characteristics* (1890) and *Village Life in China* (1899), revealed his depth of knowledge and penetrating insights. One can never forget the flood of illustration and unsuspected flashes of humor. Opening lecture: "You are doubtless aware that the main area of this great country (the eighteen provinces distinguished from the outlying border districts) is commonly known among us as China Proper. Well, let me inform you right now that about China Proper none of us really knows much, and about 'China improper' the least said the better." Equally in his religious expressions there flowed forth these subtle flashes of mind, so natural and vivid. One Sunday after his sermon in the chapel of the Peking Union Medical College, in his attending prayer the words bubbled forth: "O Lord, bless the Chinese government—if there is any." Truly the chaotic political situation of the time could give proof to the sincerity of such a petition, including its qualifying ending.

Although our year of study in Peking closed officially early in June we had the pleasure of continuing with a private teacher at China's northernmost summer resort, Pei-tai-ho. Here was begun our course of reading and memory work in the New Testament, with its attending product of interesting new meanings springing up within the setting of oriental life and language. But finally, to our resourceful young teacher, Mr. Pai (White), we had to say, "Many thanks and *tsai chien* [good-by]."

4

THE IMPERIAL CITY

*F*ROM THE FOREGOING it would appear that living in Peking had meant for us an almost total absorption in language study. Truly it encompassed immeasurably more than Mandarin drills and cultural lectures. Indeed the wonders of this ancient civilization, so concentrated in the structure and flavor of the Imperial City, ever kept beckoning us to fuller exploration.

On the day of our arrival, as we passed through the main areas of merchandising, there confronted us an attractive array of open-fronted shops with ornamental approaches richly lacquered and gilded. Beyond these inviting sights of business enterprise we entered what seemed a forbidding seclusion of residential areas. This network of narrow lanes with closely walled-in courtyards and bolted gates held the savor of mysteries within a sealed book.

If a personalized picture of Peking is to be realized, it requires confining to a few selective exposures. Bold and basic among visual impressions stands the grand physical layout of the great city, an arrangement without parallel in contemporary capitals of the world. In view of design, function, and character an early historian has given the city the apt description: "Really five cities in one." Immediately one grasps the concept of a series of concentric squares, each securely walled. The center, strictly reserved for the abode of the royal family, stood as core and heart of the Imperial Rule. While the planned formality of such a scheme may well strike one as unimaginative, the symmetrical effect is grandly impressive.

For a full panoramic view we found no skyscraper or Eiffel Tower, though "coalhill" in the Imperial City showed an attempt at elevation. Most naturally, one took recourse to the massive surrounding thirteenth-century rampart, fully fifty feet high and forty wide. While the wall was not generally accessible to the Chinese populace, it afforded us a splendid range of view and enjoyable promenade. To complete the fourteen-mile circumference of the wall presented a challenge to which we never responded. Marvelously, this ancient defensive bulwark, containing nine entrances each with double gates and bastionlike towers, remained fully intact as when constructed.

From these vantage points the eye readily caught the bold pattern of designed enclosures that widen out to great dimensions. Before us ranged the long intersecting avenues, attractive areas with artificial lakes and abundance of trees, also extensive districts of common housing and shops that seemed to offer little but their somber gray-tile rooftops. Unfailingly, of course, attention was drawn again and again to the artistic magnificence of palaces and temples— glazed roofs aglitter with yellow, green, and purple.

How could one account for this unique fivefold arrangement? The answer is found in history and circumstance. The major quadrangle, as we learned, still carried its association with alien conquest and was commonly spoken of as the Tatar or Manchu City. First the Mongolians in the thirteenth century and later the Manchurians in the seventeenth left their indelible mark on this foursquare citadel. The Tatar City with its unique arrangement of inner enclosures had been designed and appropriated as a haven of privilege and impregnable defense; it was reserved to the ruling class—the entire garrison and families of nobility, all of which lived on the bounty of the government. Manchu regulations forbade any resident to engage in business, aiming to ensure, no doubt, the dignity and integrity of the conquering race. In consequence, the extensive oblong walled-in area attached on the south side (South or Outer City) had reason to be known as the Chinese City. Its dense population and teeming marts might still be regarded as giving testimony to such long-past discriminatory origin.

The next inner square of the main city ranked as the Imperial City and continued to be so called, having for ages served as residential and official district for the ruling bureaucracy. Along with superior housing and attractive parks, its palatial governmental halls marked it as cultural and administrative hub of the farflung empire. Finally, we came to enter the innermost sanctum, yet bearing the awesome name Forbidden City. Now, since the establishment of a Republic, the ever-hovering mystery of seclusion had taken flight and the majesty of royalty was sadly fading. Yet, as we moved among gardens and terraces, courts and pavilions, palaces and temples, great halls and throne room, there lingered a pervading sense of dignity. Then, passing down the broad marble staircase with its noble carved-dragon facing and crossing the elegant "alabaster" bridge, our retreat bore uneasy thoughts of the feeble, struggling young republic.

There was yet to be noted that tiny fifth city occupying sedately a corner of the great metropolis. Arising out of modern Western impact, there had developed the Legation Quarters of the foreign powers. Apparently the same

historical necessity that brought forth international intercourse also required means of isolation and protection.
Housing the diplomatic services of several countries, along
with facilities of bank, shop, church, hotel (mainly British), it stood as a relatively independent community. Our
passport registration, banking errands, and other contacts
brought us occasionally within its guarded gates. One felt
that these diminutive ramparts carried a story of tragedy
and bravery. In the "Boxer Rebellion" attack of 1900, when
many foreign and Chinese Christians suffered massacre,
the Legation, under severe siege, endured as a place of
refuge.

To the history-minded it was interesting to realize that
from very ancient times this place had served as a local
capital, then bearing the still revered name, Yenching.
Down in the thirteenth century A.D. came the all-conquer-
ing Mongol ruler, Kublai Khan. Dethroning the Sung dynasty and standing master of the most extensive empire
ever known, he established his political and administrative center on this ground, calling it Cambaluc. A century
later arose the glorious Ming dynasty, ridding China of
the despised alien overlordship. Nanking, in the rich Yangtze Valley, became the first Ming capital. Later, the notable Emperor Yung Lo (reigned 1403–1424) restored the
dignity of the Northern capital, completely reconstructing
the city on its present grand design and scale.

Before long, we began the building up of a store of illuminating glimpses into popular customs and attitudes of
mind. Chinese New Year midnight brought an awakening
jolt by a tremendous bombardment close by. Firecrackers,
of course, go with every celebration; but this was a real
stunner. As reported, a twenty-five-dollar package had
been strung in a neighboring tree and set off with one terrific blast. Rumor traced it to Ts'ao K'un, president of the

Republic, who was giving greetings to a wealthy friend
and endowing the incoming year with peace and joy by effectively frightening off the evil spirits.

Not unlike our own Western-prevailing Christmas customs, the celebrations of the Peking populace made the
most of combining religion and festivity. Along with ancestral ceremonies of filial piety in the privacy of the
homes, thousands crowded the various temples. We mingled with the throng, observing attitudes and acts of worship, mostly by devout women. But as for youth—it all appeared like "going to the fair."

Each of the three great historic religions manifestly held
an important place in the cultural life of the capital city.
After ages of creedal struggle for ascendancy, each seemed
to have accepted a somewhat special domain in the threefold universe. In the simplified analysis of one of our early
missionary scholars, William A. P. Martin (*The Lore of
Cathay*, 1901), heaven is assigned to Buddha, hell to Taoism, and this world to Confucius. In no sense could these
spheres be considered exclusive; the Chinese mind, tending to be eclectic, can choose from each and quite possibly add elements of Christianity.

We found the architectural beauty of the great Imperial
temples a striking feature in the city's profile. Especially
was it true of the Confucian Temple with its stately structure and simple interior, so classically impressive. As to
others, within the extensive complex of connected buildings, what an astonishing variety of religious symbols and
customs!

Very revealing was our visit to the Taoist sanctum. Besides the frightful figures of evil spirits and the great
"screen of hell," many special places of prayer were afforded to meet the common daily needs. There were those
imploring for fruitage in marriage, those concerned for

business prosperity, those craving for learning. Many prayed for health, even blind beggars having their place. The most ingenious device we observed was the "healing brass horse," probably offering a process of magic for the simpleminded: just stroke the robust animal at the appropriate spot, then transfer the healthful quality to one's ailing self. A limping mother was trustfully applying the remedy to her knee. But the young daughter just had a sporting time rubbing every area of the horse's head without bothering to make connections with her own.

It would seem that Taoism (the Way), with its original high philosophy of the law of nature and later its essential deities of creator god (Jade Emperor), city god, and kitchen god, had in practice declined into superstition and mere magic. Buddhism, however, had generally retained a higher standard—holding forth the "path of escape" from suffering, while Confucianism had consistently aimed at the superior man through the fine "art of living."

Our next venture into strange ways of religious expression brought us into contact with Tibetan Buddhism at the famed Lama Temple. Following our survey of the colossal image known as the Great Buddha and hearing a litany chanted by the yellow-robed monks, we had the rare fortune of catching a glimpse of the Living Buddha. The Dalai Lama from Lhasa was then on an official call in Peking. Lamaism was commonly regarded as a corrupted form of the religion and this temple had a notorious history of still reflecting semibarbarous practices.

In the courtyard there was shaping up a display of frenzied religious dancing. In weird costume and with great rawhide snake-whips in hand, they began to leap and whirl around the pavement with fierce lashings and sharp cracks. Suddenly arose an alarm—confusion and angry shoutings! Then all attention shifted up into a spreading

tree. There, half hidden, hunched one of our Language
School fellows, busy operating a small camera. Surely it
must be an evil instrument—offense against the gods.
Down he was hauled with whips wound around him, and
he was rudely impelled into the building. We felt quite
alarmed, anxiety lying heavily upon us as to what might
be happening. Soon he reappeared, fortunately little the
worse for his experience in spite of a ruffled-up look.

How refreshing the experience of shifting the scene,
then, to the sanctuary of China's most ancient religion, the
matchless Altar of Heaven! To this place we could come,
as students of comparative religion, only with deep reverence and wonderment. These were the historic grounds of
Imperial high-priestly worship on behalf of the whole people of China. On occasion, as a pair of lone pilgrims admitted to the sanctum, Grace and I tarried for hours—just ad-
miring, absorbing, reflecting.

How could one comprehend such a scene and impart
even a shadow of its mood? An attempt made several generations ago by Chancellor Martin of the Imperial University offers a key to both pattern and spirit: "The sun in his
course looks on nothing built with hands so sublime in its
suggestions. . . . Acres of polished marble (white) rising
from all sides by flights of steps, culminate in a circular
terrace, whose roof is the vault of heaven. The divinity
there worshiped is the Ruler of the Universe and the priest
who officiates is the sovereign of the empire." Could one
help feeling that this altar, so simple in form and sublime
in purpose, was speaking with a voice direct from the
ages? This ancient civilization of the East probably had a
concept of the universal God of all the earth and offered to
him sacrificial worship—a concept later sustained by the
wisdom of Confucius.

Down to the latest emperor this traditional ceremonial

sacrifice was solemnly perpetuated. Once a year, following
a season of fasting in the Hall of Silence, the Son of
Heaven performed this high-priestly service. Even Yüan
Shih-k'ai, as president of the Republic, proposed continuing the practice—an idea not readily accepted by the enlightened public. And yet, in the presence of this memorable altar, one could hardly forbear the wish that in some
worthy way such a symbolic lesson of worship might direct
the minds of the masses to the Eternal Sovereign. How
much better this would be than burning incense sticks before images in shabby Buddhist temples! Precious to our
memory is that moonlight evening when a group of us from
the school gathered on the Altar to sing hymns of praise to
our Lord and Master.

Still another unusual and enriching experience we found
in the little chapel of the Russian Orthodox Mission. Their
three-hour midnight Easter service easily held us in the
charm of curiosity and reverence. So tightly packed was
the chapel, with everyone standing, that we practically
formed an immovable mass. The ornate chancel setting, li-
turgical ceremonies, towering Russian high priest with
long white beard and full regalia—all these restored to our
minds childhood conceptions of Biblical worship. Truly
blessed were the Sacrament of bread and wine, the holy
kiss, the heavenly chants with a Chinese priest touching
low bass, and finally, divine blessing hovering over us all
as the priest wove among the crowd swinging high his
censer of incense.

Of course, none could miss opportunities available in the
North for other significant historical observations. The
spirit of Chinese history kept calling us out to visit various
renowned and memorable places inseparably associated
with the Imperial City though far beyond its confines. By
special tours (group-organized), we indulged in the thrills

of treading the ancient ramparts of China's Great Wall, of roaming among the delicately designed architectural structures of the Summer Palace Gardens, and of spending a reverential day (and glorious night under glittering stars) within the expansive and monumental layout constituting the Imperial Tomb of the famed Emperor Yung Lo—greatest of the Ming rulers and builder of modern Peking.

Unmistakably, we kept noting situations in China's capital that reflected a composite of the times, though occasionally we savored sharply here the old and there the new. Among impressive examples, we were enabled on the one hand to witness the fantastically elaborate funeral rites of the late minister of interior under the monarchy, and then, in turn, had the privilege of visiting the modernized army encampment of the new Capital Garrison with its progressive leadership and unique type of administration.

Grasping the rare opportunity of observing memorial rites appropriated to Imperial officialdom, we sought early for a favorable position among the assembling mass. There, before us, on the broad Hattaman Avenue stood four imposing pavilions (temporary bamboo structures). These were openly displaying elegant furnishings and rich embroideries belonging to the family of the deceased. There were also convenient tearooms, with tables and chairs, and a small shrine with lighted candles. A pair of life-sized lions (evergreen) stood guarding the estate, which had on one corner a pagodalike monument and on the other the magnificent bier.

For fully an hour and a half our eyes remained set upon this passing parade of sights seldom seen. Really, the funeral bier (catafalque), a complex of red-lacquered poles upon which the coffin was borne, was so tremendous that a company of sixty-four men was required to carry it.

Ahead walked the men of the clan in their white, coarse overgarments of mourning and behind came the women in carriages and sedan chairs. Several live animals followed: a couple of richly bedecked camels and a pair of white horses. The continuing train carried an array of silken umbrellas with gaudy floating banners, quantities of artificial flowers, shrubs, and trees carried by coolies, paper figures of domestic animals and fowls, shrines containing miniature men and women—and finally, the climax, an actual-size black cardboard automobile being pushed along by hand.

Oddly, the procession was enlivened by the interspersing of three different bands (instrumental), which were stronger on volume than harmony. Also a company of ragged beggars trudged along, assured that the occasion would provide ample handouts of food. Here and there showers of paper money were generously scattered along the way.

Presumably this abounding variety of artificial objects was then to be burned at the grave, symbols of all the comforts and blessings to attend the spirit of the departed. To us it appeared that all this elaborate pageantry was somehow woven around two objectives: display of elegance and wealth to denote social rank and honor, and symbolism, by earthly endowments, of a propitious passing into the spirit world.

If the funeral customs we witnessed may be looked upon as laden with ostentation and superstition, thus representing decadent tradition, then the new-style military camp later visited clearly demonstrated the elements of emerging progress.

Several months previously a strange military-political maneuver had been enacted in our midst; and we, barely initiated into Chinese politics, grasped only slightly its implications. Suddenly out of the northwest an army appeared which ousted the official Peking garrison and made President Ts'ao K'un virtually a prisoner. The little-known "people's general," Fêng Yü-hsiang, had expeditiously set himself guard over the capital city. In this, a new light appeared. A new hand was raised against the corruption and futility that plagued the infant republic.

Plans for bringing the general to address the Language School miscarried, but by invitation our entire body (forty) was privileged to visit the camp (our first auto ride in China). What an exhilarating experience to find in a Chinese army of 300,000 about 12,000 acknowledged Christians. Just a week before, some of our friends attended the riverside service when 1,113 had received baptism upon profession. The Chinese evangelist (Swedish missionary) spoke highly of the sincerity of these men and the cleanness of their habits.

In the absence of the "Christian General," a splendid group of junior officers showed us around. Modesty, cleanliness, simplicity, and efficiency marked the character of the camp. What a leap from the customary lazy, slouchy, plundering armies! This camp was remarkably clean and throbbing with constructive activity.

Aside from his military drill, every soldier worked daily at a trade. Building after building we found buzzing with the simple crafts: cotton-spinning and weaving; producing socks, towels, rugs; making garments (with Singer sewing machines); cobbling shoes; carpentering and smithing. From the soap factory we each carried off by courtesy a fragrant cake. Inescapably from the large signboard leaped the words, "If a man will not work, neither shall he eat." A glimpse at the neat little school for the wives and daughters of officers, a brief talk and prayer by the guiding lieutenant, and we were off. It was a day of good cheer.

5

ENGULFED IN REVOLUTION

$\mathcal{U}$ PON RETURNING to Hangchow in September, 1924, we came again upon the thriving and ordered aspect of the riverside campus. Could it be sedately smiling at the temper of the times? Oh, no, hardly that. Uncertainty and alarm kept the social atmosphere charged, as daily rumors and rumblings told of political maneuvers and military clashes. It all bespoke a patient waiting for fall college opening.

In Peking warnings had been sounded of travel difficulties. Nevertheless the "Express" served us well to Nanking and then the Yangtze steamer took us to Shanghai, the southern line of the railway being commandeered for troops. Five foreign gunboats standing alert in the Nanking harbor gave evidence of prevailing tension. Yet, in spite of these forebodings, how pleasurably the "Mighty Yangtze"—with sources in the high ranges of Tibet, regarded as the swiftest river in the world, and navigable over a thousand miles—afforded a peaceful voyage on one of its fine vessels. Then again, how reassuringly our Shanghai-Hangchow railway shuttled its passengers as if everything were normal.

Scarcely a fortnight passed before the suspense broke.

Civil clashes began churning our area into popular turmoil and imminent civil war. Skirmishes were occurring here and there for weeks, as massive troop movements kept pouring alongside the campus. The governor of Chekiang, General Lu Yung-hsiang, a man held in high esteem for his progressive spirit, was judiciously withdrawing his forces toward the Shanghai area, which he controlled. From the South entered the scourge of the less disciplined army of General Sun Chuan-fang, military governor of Fukien Province. Sun, a Northerner, native of Shantung, ambitious and harsh, advanced with the objective of making himself master of the five East China provinces, thereby commanding the revenues and exercising power in Peking.

While as yet the military rampage had scarcely begun, already general panic reigned among the populace. To former forebodings fuel was added by a strange intervening event on the very day of General Sun's arrival. Hangchow's famous thousand-year-old Thunder Peak Pagoda on the edge of West Lake, long reduced to a mere towering core, crumbled into a mound of rubble. Surely it meant an ill omen!

Surprisingly, after six weeks our situation became relatively pacified, so that the college managed to open and carry on with even a record enrollment, but accompanied also with a rash of new disturbing forces less tangible than clashing armies. As to the unwelcome Northern governorship, this burden the city and province were destined to endure for a couple of strenuous years.

In the fall of 1926 we were dealt a terrible stroke. Already pressed by the emergence of the new Nationalist army advancing from the South, General Sun began to move his forces northward. Immediately, the mayor of Hangchow, also civil governor of Chekiang, took the bold and hasty step of declaring provincial independence. Hsia

Dzao was a native Chekiang man, moved by strong Nationalist sympathies, but he was not equipped with adequate military force. Speedily the warlord returned, crushing the rebellion and summarily executing the mayor.

These were tense and tragic times for all of us in Hangchow. Before the final departure of the Northern armies more than a year later, the entire countryside suffered their ravages and a portion of the city experienced wholesale looting. Local people had fled by the thousands to seek the safety of the Shanghai International Settlement, and as to missionaries, many were devoting themselves to Red Cross service.

At the same time we became acutely aware of a new charge pervading the atmosphere. The Nationalist Revolution was here! The marching, liberating armies had already laden the wind with an advance spearhead of fiery ideas. However, the revolutionary hopes that we so deeply shared had scarcely prepared us for its negative and hostile aspects. Indeed, it was quite shocking to be caught up suddenly in a wave of antiforeign agitation and antichristian sentiment!

Christmas Day of 1924 has become especially notable in memory. Our awaited prospective house and home, the first since marriage, was now freshly renovated and ready for Christmas breakfast. In keeping with the joy and hope of the day, we joined the celebration by the Christian community of the sixtieth anniversary of the Presbyterian Church in Hangchow (the first church founded in the city). Then arose, from the seeming calm, a waft of disturbing news; a demonstration of a different nature was on schedule for the morrow, marking the rise of the antichristian movement. This parade, staged by students and some officials, carried placards and shouted slogans denouncing Chinese Christians as "running dogs" of Western imperialism.

Within the student unions emerged radical leaders. While government institutions afforded the hotbed, our Christian schools were likewise affected. Also teachers, officials, and writers, in fact many segments of society, were becoming aroused and vocal against "oppressive warlords" and "exploiting foreign interests." Months later the "May 30th incident" in Shanghai in 1925 kindled an explosion of antiforeignism. After trouble had arisen in a Japanese cotton mill, police faced a critical situation of student riot; and by firing into the mob, under orders of a British officer, they killed several students. By this regrettable action and the attendant martyrdom of the murdered students, the entire country became inflamed.

In the face of these winds of change and storm, one had to scan the background and probe the patterns, so as to formulate a capsule concept of China's political complexities. Politically, the country stood divided between two rival forces, neither exercising authority beyond its own orbit. The conservative North, with formal governmental machinery in Peking, was recognized by the powers; but being farcical and corrupt, it could be held together only by a flimsy balance of warlords. On the other hand, the revolutionary South, having headquarters in Canton, possessed a store of democratic ideals and a progressive program but was without status and had scant military power. Its strength lay in the vigorous flow of propaganda that broadcast the seeds of new ideas and hopes. What little of order prevailed throughout the country lay in the hands of local warlords or regional military cliques.

The man at this time occupying the office of the presidency and the historic palaces was the infamous General Ts'ao K'un—elected through bribery and supported by Northern generals. Since the formation of the Republic (October, 1911), Peking had endured a succession of seven presidents. Beginning hopefully with Dr. Sun Yat-sen as provisional president and then being followed by the strong man Yüan Shih-k'ai, who had untimely monarchical ambitions and an early demise (1916), the high office of state thereafter provided meager leadership.

Two "old order" generals stood out as dominating the Northern scene. Representing the more scholarly type was Wu P'ei-fu, holding a degree under the old classical system and on occasion withdrawing from public life to a quiet monastery. The less refined Chang Tso-lin made his emergence from Manchuria, having risen to power from an early career as a brigand.

In the South a totally different spirit prevailed because of the close contact with Western civilization. The Southern Confederacy at Canton, with Sun Yat-sen at its head, claimed to be the legal government of China. Here, as early as 1912, the Kuomintang was formed, combining the several revolutionary parties and formulating the Three Principles of the People. The Kuomintang aimed at national unity, popular government, and social welfare. These principles of national consciousness and progressive society had taken wings and were literally permeating the country.

The Kuomintang (literally, Revolutionary Party) in original form could not be called Marxist either in theory or in aim; being cast on moderate lines, its appeal was to academic, professional, and mercantile groups. It was, however, reformist in spirit and nationalist in temper, leading later to the rise of an extremist left wing (1923). (Strangely enough, the Chinese Communist Party had its original cells in the National University of Peking in 1919.)

Out of this, one could establish the connecting link with General Fêng Yü-hsiang's garrison in Peking, previously described. This phenomenal military camp proved to be no less than the People's Army (Kuominchun). The People's Party (Kuomintang), by winning over a Northern general, had thereby extended its arm and laid a hand upon the capital city (a venture understood by few persons, including myself). Little was achieved substantially, however, since in a brief time the "Christian General" tactfully withdrew his army to the northwest, when Wu P'ei-fu, his former superior, sprang from retirement to crush the "renegade." Apparently the new national spirit was catching fire throughout the land; but the hope for cooperation between the Kuomintang and the Peking military clique was totally futile. Apparently General Fêng Yü-hsiang, alone among warlords of the time, could discern the coming political current and had in fact invited Sun Yat-sen by telegram to come to the North and confer with Northern military leaders.

Naturally, we found ourselves too close to the scene for any clear perspectives. This was the case in spite of the high-quality news media—*North China Daily News* (British) and *China Press* (American), published in Shanghai. Local involvements often beclouded the picture. For who, amid clusters of swirling bamboo, envisions the pattern of the grove? The great fact stood: the regenerating force of the Nationalist Revolution was giving hope for new China —whatever the attending disruptions.

With eyes focused upon Canton, fountainhead of the Nationalist spirit, one could chart emerging developments. As early as 1921, at the disbanding of the National Parliament in Peking, the Kuomintang members proceeded to restore in the South the "true Chinese Republic," with their undaunted revolutionary leader, Sun Yat-sen, again elected president. But Sun, being more of an ideologist than a practical administrator, felt the movement in urgent need of help from abroad. Upon suffering rebuff from the most likely powers, United States, Great Britain, and Japan, he turned to the "rising star" of Soviet Russia for support. Here he readily found not only a wealth of revolutionary experience but advice waiting for export.

Thus originated the very significant liaison between the Kuomintang and the aspiring Chinese Communist Party. Communists, though admitted as individuals, were required to pledge loyalty to the Kuomintang. First, in 1923, the Canton Government welcomed as its political adviser the astute and widely experienced Michael Borodin. Then, in 1924, when Russia still maintained official relations with Peking, a sizable group of Russian specialists arrived in Canton for boosting the political propaganda and tuning up the military instruction. In very short order, the formerly loose-knit Kuomintang had undergone a thorough tightening up and the struggling army had achieved a new unity and strength.

In the spring of 1925 we were encouraged by reports of a promising new revolutionary leader emerging in Canton. Shortly before this, Sun Yat-sen, having been in feeble health, made his last journey to Peking in hopes of some form of compromise. There the venerated Father of the Republic died, leaving an unfinished task and a vacant chair. The dashing young general who picked up the mantle of leadership was the then-little-known Chiang Kai-shek. He was credited by the foreign press in Shanghai as combining forceful personality and administrative ability, while we of Hangchow attributed to him also the sound qualities of a Chekiang native. Already he was heading the newly formed Whampoa Military Academy for training the People's Model Army, being assisted by the brilliant military strategist Marshal Galen (Russian) as chief instructor.

The following spring, then, brought the launching of General Chiang's victorious Northern Expedition. It reached us in Hangchow nearly a year later. Steadily, province after province was coming under the blue-and-white banner of the Kuomintang—actually with a minimum of fighting. Practically everywhere, these patriotic and disciplined forces, with advance corps of political agents, received the greeting and cooperation of the civilian population. The Revolution kept advancing: Changsha, July 12; Hankow, September 7; Foochow, December 3; and Hangchow, February 18, 1927.

Meanwhile, life on the campus had its constant flares of excitement and disturbing uncertainties. No more obtained the traditional ivory-tower concept of classical education! In December, 1926 (again, Christmas Day), students set themselves to digging trenches on our grounds while cannonade poured forth from our hilltops. Marshal Sun Chuanfang, determined to hold back the Nationalist flood, had placed us squarely in the path of military movements. Fully two hundred thousand soldiers permeated the district, streaming daily along the campus edge, giving ample occasion for alarm and fears of depredations. Far and wide, villages were suffering frightful ravages, many helpless refugees finding shelter and relief in our college buildings. Only the mile-wide Chien Tang River separated this occupying Northernist military horde from an advance division of the Nationalist army. Most of the students, responding to urgent parental calls due to our exposed location, quickly departed for home—much to our relief.

The question of evacuating foreign women and children had to be faced by all in Hangchow, especially Americans, as the Consulate allowed little choice. Grace, having gone

to Shanghai (although much against her will) and having
endured a miserable week of refugeeing, felt the chances
in Hangchow to be better. So she came home, remaining
the only foreign woman "out on the Hill" and providing
hostess services to all of us.

After a stretch of eighteen perilous and tragic days,
Sun's forces began withdrawal, practically acknowledging
defeat at the hands of the hostile populace. The militarist
had lost his foothold. The long-burdened people had
caught the vision of hope and a promise. The permeating
antiwarlord propaganda and innate yearnings for a new order kept carrying their victorious march ahead of the advancing Nationalist army. We too felt that our dreams
were about to reap reward.

The hour struck on February 18, 1927. Chiang Kai-shek's
youthful warriors entered Hangchow, claiming for the
commander his native province. From our heights we
spied their first deploying companies, with light artillery,
coming along the river road and then appropriating our
athletic field as an inviting spot for them to step aside and
take ease. Here, several of the college missionary staff, led
by Frank Price, undertook to offer a greeting word, which
to our amazement met shocking rebuff. Hard-worn uniforms and straw sandals seemed to add dignity to these
youthful soldiers; and so also their independent spirit permitted no fraternization with Westerners in China.

From the commanding officer poured a flood of indignation: "Why have you grabbed this mountain and made it a
seat of foreign learning?" Efforts to explain that we had
taken nothing away but were here only to give, and expressed hopes that the Chinese would very soon be able to
carry all the educational responsibilities, fell on deaf ears.
Likewise, acknowledging the injustice of foreign treaty
rights evoked no favorable response, only the adamant

mood: "We shall restore China's sovereign rights; we shall vindicate our national honor; you have robbed and shamed us."

Such confrontation and condemnation was enough to leave one stunned. It was also an awakener, a challenge to examine our mission and role in China in an era of aroused nationalism. Yes, for such a time we had worked and prayed, and we had sought to lay Christian foundations upon which to build. Now we began to see that the road to reconciliation between a sophisticated West and a humiliated China would be rocky and long. Who would be equal to it?

While our depopulated campus remained relatively undisturbed, everything within the city broke loose in a wild orgy of celebration and revolutionary propaganda. Proclamations, posters, and torchlight parades all hammered upon the same themes and slogans: "Strike down militarism," "Down with foreign imperialism," "Away with the foreign devils." The wave of extremism let loose caused labor stoppage, rice riots, and mob disorder.

After a few days of judicious seclusion at home, we (Grace and I) ventured down the road to the railway terminal, Zakow, strategic south entrance to the city. There, confronted with a barrage of wall posters, we stood appraising their significance. Especially were we amused at the odd caricature of the ousted warlord, Sun Chuan-fang, posted upside down. "Who are you?" spoke a voice beside us, a neat young officer sizing us up. A courtesy nod, and I explained, "We belong to the American college over on that hill." "But what is your nationality?" came the sharp demand. "Oh, yes, I am Canadian by birth with residence in the United States and am serving in the American college." "Well—O.K., then," and a puzzled look. With a sharp gesture for us to be on the move came his parting retort:

"But we do hate the British."

Not many weeks later, this rumble of hatred and hostil-
ity began to take the form of direct threats. We became
aware of the critical turn when a group of soldiers passing
on the road brusquely announced: "You foreigners—when
this war is over we shall come back and kill all of you."
What could be the meaning of this?

March 24 brought the climactic jolt. Communications totally disrupted, rumors had it that the Chinese section of
Shanghai had fallen to the Nationalists, with high tension
prevailing in the foreign settlements. Both British and
American consuls had earlier taken emergency precautions and sent instructions for the safety of nationals in interior places. The head of our physics laboratory kept on
the watch, holding contact with the outside by means of
his self-constructed radio. Receivers clapped to his ears,
suddenly he caught a special message: "Willie is very ill,
operation necessary, attention family concerned!" This was
repeated several times—yes, it must be the official call. All
must evacuate as speedily as possible to the protected settlements.

The crisis had arisen not in Shanghai but in Nanking.
There the extremist element of the Nationalist army had
run totally amok. To stop the horrible rampage of abuse,
violence, rape, and murder inflicted upon missionaries and
other foreigners, British and American gunboats had to be
set into action. International tension having hit the explosive point, could anyone gauge the consequences?

Fortunately, in Hangchow sanity prevailed. Responsible
officials held little in common with the inflaming rantings
of the Propaganda Division. Foreign residents were urged
to remain and protection was offered; but our Chinese co-
workers thought it best that we all leave. On a special passenger coach, attached to a slow-moving and incredibly

packed troop train, our foreign group of forty managed to reach Shanghai. This was arranged for us by courtesy of the military commander and with his guarantee for safety.

Deep in the night we drew into the Shanghai South Station, where in a hushed manner we were received by a few select friends. Their relief seemed to be greater than ours. As yet we felt reluctant to join the refugee millions, not having fully caught their mood of apprehension. The sight of French soldiers sternly manning the barricades at the Concession entrance and a company of alert American marines on hand raised the question: Was all this assuring or alarming?

This was Shanghai! Next morning we realized that the great port city lay in the throes of extreme tension. How shocking to hear that a tremendous mass meeting, up to a hundred thousand, had been gathered at the South Station (located in the Chinese City) on the day before. Fiery propagandists were flinging out the slogans: "Down with the foreigners," "Take back the Concessions." So gravely did the international authorities view the crisis that they seemed disposed to negotiate the issue of the International Settlement. At the same time, the large accumulation of American and British ships in the harbor anticipated an emergent necessity of evacuating the entire body of their nationals. So much was depending upon the temper and direction of the Nationalist movement at this crucial stage.

Our refugeeing in Shanghai, along with the thousands of others so grateful for order, shelter, and bunks, proved for us to be only a matter of weeks. The Presbyterian Mission of East China, in speedy consultation concluded that only a few key men should remain on the field during this uncertain time. With our first furlough (after five years of service) nearly due, obviously we belonged to the group to be sent home. It was a reluctant departure from a people

and a service with which we had found identification and
to which we might never be able to return.

Blessedly, Shanghai, "haven of refuge," was spared international conflict, but the Chinese City sadly bore the
agony of brief civil war. The revolutionary armies, having
crossed the Yangtze, kept pressing northward, headed for
the strongholds of Generals Wu P'ei-fu and Chang Tso-lin.
However, more fundamental than the military aspect, the
overriding question of the real character of the Revolution had been asked and was being answered. Was China
to be governed by the moderate wing of the Kuomintang
or by the extremist left and by the Communist Party? Here
lay a deep concern for our Christian missions, for the foreign governments, and for the mass of thinking Chinese.

Much could be learned of the situation by a look at what
was being brewed at the Nationalist headquarters at Hankow. Here the staff of Russian advisers was now supplemented by more than five hundred returned students with
a year's study at the Sun Yat-sen University, Moscow.
More and more the radical elements were moving up into
the saddle, with earmarks of a projected Communist take-
over. Presumably this accounted for some of the threats of
violence to foreigners in Hangchow and the outrages of
pillage and murder in Nanking. Also, with the General Labor Union in Shanghai being under the direction of Communists (the leader being Cho En-lai), the total life of the
city could be paralyzed at a stroke.

The commander-in-chief of the army had no such mind
or mood. Chiang Kai-shek, never on easy terms with the
Communist advisers, had little taste for their political
schemes and radical tactics. Instead of troublesome labor
unions and provocations of foreigners, his objectives were
stable government, commercial prosperity, and cooperative foreign relations. Sharply disciplining unruly elements

of the army and directing his attention to mass uprisings in Shanghai, he definitely fixed the course of the Revolution. The Communist-led labor movement was crushed with a stern severity that left no doubt of purpose but raised questions of wisdom. (One of our fine students became a victim.)

Next step was to set up a new government in Nanking, canceling out the Hankow group and putting the Russian advisers to heel. So ended the "marriage of convenience" between the Chinese Kuomintang and the Communist International. (This situation I explained in my article, "The Triumph of the Nationalists in China," *New York Times* Current History, January, 1929.)

Catching up with developments at the college, we learned that control had been placed in the hands of our Chinese colleagues. How gratifying to have such men of academic qualification and Christian caliber. Andrew Wu, our dean, assumed leadership and inspired confidence. He had behind him a worthy record: graduate of both Hangchow and College of Wooster, war service in France with Chinese Labor Corps, and later his degree from Princeton Theological Seminary. Truly, the college was not only surviving the Revolution, but it had become an integral part of it by transfer of responsibility to Chinese leadership.

We also became aware of other significant happenings in and around Hangchow, especially the experiences of one of our fellow missionaries, Stephen Sturton, M.D. Remarkably, he was enabled to join the Red Cross Medical Unit of the Nationalist forces. Steve ranked as one of the able young surgeons on the staff of the British hospital, and as our personal medical attendant displayed both brilliance and tenderness.

Since the brunt of antiforeignism was falling upon the British, the noted C. M. S. Hospital became a convenient target. Several misguided patriots in the provincial government forced a take-over, to have the hospital "restored to the Chinese." The responsible native Christian doctor, with no foreigner at hand, could not prevent this official action or stop the subsequent removal of much valuable equipment.

Into this situation, early in 1928, stepped Dr. Sturton. Just returned from furlough in England and having been newly appointed administrator of the hospital, he found no place to set foot. To his sensitive spirit came presently a clear call to a special mission. "I must go to the wounded and dying," he felt. Specifically, the appeal was voiced by a personal friend, none less than the distinguished surgeon general of the Chinese army, Dr. W. S. New, a man of Harvard training and of well-grounded Christian faith.

Attended by Chinese escort, Dr. Sturton entered the embattled areas where casualties mounted high and there began service in the Base Hospital for the Seriously Wounded. The movement of military headquarters to this base soon brought the presence of General and Madame Chiang Kai-shek, who became so impressed with the British surgeon that they chose him for their personal physician. A binding friendship ensued.

Could the humanitarian and spiritual fruits of Dr. Sturton's three-month stint in the Chinese Red Cross ever be measured? It was a simple and natural missionary act. On the basis of a related story, the puzzled general of Confucian background was asking, "How can a man who is being shut out of his own hospital turn the occasion into such a self-giving service?" Replied the Madame, "This is Christianity." By direct intervention from the "highest authority" the Hangchow C. M. S. Hospital was in due time restored to the Mission and into the hands of its rightful administrator.

6

CONSTRUCTIVE NATIONALISM

*W*E RETURNED to China eagerly in September, 1928, sensing the prospects of a newly unified nation with stable government and progressive outlook. Before us stood the promise of a challenging era—a field day for Christian education. Mission institutions had well earned recognition for providing the pattern and setting the standards for a modern educational system in China. Hangchow Christian College we could envision now as entering into the full flower of her high mission. In this we aimed to share.

Behind us lay a rewarding furlough year at the University of Chicago. I had been pursuing political studies, sitting, as it were, at the feet of the masters. Most outstanding, for my interests, were Charles E. Merriam as prime American scholar in political theory and Quincy Wright, the noted authority on international law and American diplomacy. Then also, as the newest dish on the menu, the brilliant Harold D. Laswell opened the uncharted wilderness of psychological phenomena in politics.

Notably, in family matters, we enjoyed a most enriching event—the gift of a precious babe. Virginia May started her travels early—being almost directly launched on her first trip to China, carried snugly in a wicker basket and cooing responsively to attentive voyagers.

Proceeding on our way, we were not unaware of a perplexing situation having developed at the college. It arose out of a new set of governmental regulations. The Nationalist government was undertaking to bring all private educational institutions into the broadly accepted national policy by a system of registration that imposed standard requirements and certain restrictions for obtaining official recognition. All mission schools faced the crucial question of religious freedom. Could they retain their Christian character? Grave fears had arisen among responsible trustees in America and governing boards on the field, while others contended that no essential liberties would be lost. Amid these divisions and uncertainties the Board of Control, awaiting clarification, had resorted to declaring Hangchow Christian College "temporarily closed for reorganization."

Since our campus obviously would be in a state of inactivity for 1928–1929, we welcomed a tentative assignment to our Mission academy in Soochow, where the knotty problem of registration was already being satisfactorily adjusted.

We found the time-honored city of Soochow to be closely akin to Hangchow. The traditional and familiar classic adage clearly read: "Above is heaven and below are Soo and Hang." Along with notable families and lovely private gardens went vigorous crafts and shrewd merchandising—with also extensive Christian institutions, especially the American Methodist Soochow University and adjoining hospital.

Into this fruitful year of service and fellowship entered, for us, another great blessing. To the question, What is really so special about Soochow? came the reply, "Oh, its pretty girls." To our "China girl," Mary Frances, was given the special privilege of being born in Soochow.

The college reopened in September, 1929, under a reorganized administration and, with what to many seemed shocking—the word "Christian" dropped out of the official name! Could this mean a departure from its founded purpose and established character, or new bottles for old wine?

The primary aim and requirement of reorganization called for putting all levels of Mission education under Chinese leadership. Specifically this meant that heads of institutions must be Chinese and there must be a majority of Chinese on controlling boards, surely a moderate requirement for meeting the needs of an awakened and sensitive nationalism. And in accord with progressive policy emerging in the Mission, the time was fully ripe for shifting controls to Chinese Christian leadership. "Indigenous" became the word. Had we not been engaged in the task of leadership training since the establishing of Hangchow Presbyterian College in 1897?

To Baen E. Lee (class of 1910) fell the honor of becoming the first Chinese president of Hangchow College—replacing Dr. Robert F. Fitch, the energetic promoter. Scholastically and spiritually he measured well, holding advanced degrees from the University of Chicago and New York University, being experienced in both business matters and literary pursuits (English editor at Shanghai Commercial Press), and having a solid grounding in the Christian faith. Here was the man for the place and the hour.

President Lee was inaugurated in 1931, after achieving full registration for the college. Already for three years he had served in an acting capacity, demonstrating his concern and ability while bearing major responsibilities in the ongoing reorganization. At this time also, for sharing administrative burdens, was added the service of Dr. Robert J. McMullen.

Again the campus throbbed in an atmosphere of promise. Fired by the challenge of innovation and rising standards, a new spirit of dedication and expansion took over, yielding a greatly strengthened teaching staff and immediate construction of two urgently needed buildings. As a gift from the Alumni Association there arose the attractive Alumni Library, richly endowed with a rare collection of Chinese classics. By special Mission funds came the realization of the dreamed-for Science Hall with all its up-to-date equipment. The achievement of these earlier planned additions for the expansion of the arts and sciences adequately qualified us as an acceptable liberal arts college.

Among the special attractions that greatly increased the body of students was our new series of practical courses: theory and practice of teaching, commerce and banking, industrial chemistry, and the like. Most novel was the opening of the civil engineering department. The energetic Chinese director (trained and experienced in the U.S.A.), a highly qualified and practical-minded engineer, forthwith began fitting out a troop of highway surveyors and bridge designers.

Actually, these well-conceived developments pointed toward the attainment of the status of a university, to be composed of three fully equipped departments (colleges): liberal arts, commerce, and engineering. And yet beyond this lay the prospect of a correlated program with the several East China Christian institutions of higher learning.

Now, academically, the college was riding the tide in serving the needs of society. But what became of our distinctive Christian witness? This had been the controversial issue in the registration problem. Seemingly contrary to the original purpose and practice of all Christian schools, Government regulations forbade the requiring of students to take the basic course in Bible and attend weekday chapel and Sunday worship services. Indeed, cutting out these major means of imparting religious knowledge to everyone and of presenting the message of evangelism could well appear to be severing the umbilical cord of Christian education. Opinions had clashed sharply. Yet, in the face of China's revolutionary spirit and challenging educational opportunities, a broader view began to emerge. Actually, nothing was being denied except the element of compulsion. Everything could be offered freely. Perhaps the New China was teaching us something about freedom of choice and the positive side of learning. And, by becoming an integral part of China's own educational system, could we not serve the better in permeating students and community with Christian ideals and principles?

The resulting new statement of aim (acceptable to Missions and Government) read: "The purpose of the founders in conducting Hangchow College is to carry out the general aims of the Nationalist Government; also in the Christian spirit of love and sacrifice, to prepare men with the highest qualifications, intellectual ability, and practical training to meet the needs of society." In this way, both the aim and the status of the college were clarified. Essentially we were marching with the times, as the early thirties had caught us all up in the wave of "Rethinking Missions." In the critical reappraisal (covering also Burma, India, Japan), China became the major objective and occasion for considerable storm on both sides of the Pacific. With William E. Hocking (Harvard professor of philosophy) leading the Commission of Appraisal, their report held the title: "A Laymen's Inquiry After One Hundred Years."

All of us came under the hammer—foreign mission boards, home churches, and field workers. "Update missions in Asia" was the call. Not only methods were challenged, but even the nature of the message. How relevant and effective was the mission work within the changing conditions and moods? For us, specifically, it was a question of how to relate education and evangelism. To many of us (as to the critics) the answer was found in close connection with our interpretation of the Christian faith in Asian lands. Presenting it as a way of life and of thinking seemed to offer a key. Surely Christianity may be conceived of as personal response and commitment to the sovereign love of God and the spirit of Jesus Christ as the motive force of life and of rightful relationships. The teaching and exemplifying of Christianity would find many avenues of expression. Our college seal called it "Truth and Love."

Among the many new features turning up on the campus, probably the most cheering was the arrival of girls' faces and voices in the halls on the Dragon Hills. We had gone coeducational. This progressive and timely outreach, along with adding a fresh flavor and charm, produced a healthy spirit of social companionship and academic competition. Since even at this stage of social change family customs still afforded scant opportunity for adult boy-girl acquaintance, parents as well as youth welcomed the forward step. Furthermore, in line with the emerging feminine role in public affairs, these girls plunged into a variety of specialties—including teaching, commerce, and even politics.

Naturally, patriotic exercises and instruction obtained high rating. Every morning the bugle call brought the assemblage for sunrise flag-raising and salute, usually followed by setting-up exercises or some form of military drill. Political indoctrination assumed a prime place. Party principles and program had to be instilled into the student mind by a Government instructor, a course of study allowing no freedom of choice. Each Monday a special assembly ceremony was required. After the singing of the national anthem came the ritual of bowing three times before the portrait of the revered revolutionist and Father of the Republic, Sun Yat-sen. Then followed the paying of solemn attention to the reading of Sun's last expressed wish, which conveyed his "Will for the People." Thus were cultivated and set the Nationalist revolutionary aims for China's reconstruction.

Religious practice no doubt presented the sharpest change. Unlike political necessities, religion had been shifted to the category of the elective; and in the mood of the time, it seemed to offer no great attractions. Actually, Bible instruction was still permitted in the curriculum without restraint, worship and prayer services were openly conducted, and personal witness in a private way retained complete freedom. But participation in our religious offerings depended entirely upon personal interest and voluntary choice. Nothing was required.

In these new circumstances, compared with previous conditions, we appeared to be experiencing a great slump that might have been reckoned a disaster. In faith, we took it as a challenge. New methods were undertaken, especially the stress upon Christian Student Fellowships for informal Bible study and shared thinking. Notable speakers brought to the pulpit drew increasing numbers to the Sunday worship and to the weekday chapel exercises. Gradually church life began to thrive again. The records tell that in the 1933–1934 school year 126 were newly added to the college church, while interest in Bible study as a regular course raised class enrollment to 140.

Prospective careers and services of our graduates also pointed to a new trend. Notably, in the past, Hangchow Christian College had achieved an outstanding record in rearing servants for the church. Of 218 graduates, up to the middle twenties, forty-eight served in the ministry and ninety-four became teachers—chiefly in Christian schools. The new era was opening broader fields for Christian impact upon society, in commerce, construction, industry, and government service.

While at this stage we had come to realize that the direct motive of most students coming to Hangchow College was to gain the advantages of modern education after Western patterns, we nevertheless banked strongly on the pervading environment. Even if, to many students, Bible courses and chapel services might be regarded as something incidental or to be totally avoided, yet we had reason to hope and believe that the Christian spirit of our campus life might become for some the most enduring element in their education. This was our faith and our prayer.

Obviously, of overriding significance in the whole of Chinese society and of particular interest in our political science department was the stabilized and progressive character of the National Government. There was no more the Imperial Rule by edict; gone was the anemic and unworkable First Republic! China was advancing into the new era of governmental organization and function which would provide modern executive direction, representative law-making, and administrative responsibility.

After much fighting and strategic bargaining to gain dominion over the northern warlords, on October 10, 1928, the Kuomintang, under the strong man Chiang Kai-shek, became the established "National Government of the Republic of China," with declared objectives of unity and modernization. Establishing the capital in Nanking meant withdrawing from the intrigues of the North and identifying with the vigorous commercial and industrial enterprises of the East China coast. A new progressiveness!

One could not fail to sense this refreshing new political atmosphere. A spirit of liberalism was taking over. Modern standards of efficiency were set forth and practiced. Notably, such new patterns particularly characterized the Western-trained staffs in Nanking and abounded in the halls of Government-maintained universities. All across the country the Kuomintang Government began to win esteem and inspire public confidence.

Outstanding among the new undertakings was the advancement in public education. Modern methods of learning were introduced, beginning in many areas at the primary level, and mounting the scale up to research institutions. Who, among the literate, did not know of the founding of the National Research Academy—the *Academia Sinica*. This multidivision research center, comprising ten different institutes in the physical and social sciences, produced such achievements as the startling archaeological excavations that presented to the world the "Peking man."

Modern transportation marked a close second in the timely strides of social progress. Up to this time, almost unbelievably, waterways had provided China's major means of travel and transport. Apart from the Shanghai-Peking line, with its extension to Hangchow, practically no railways were in operation, while highways remained almost unknown. In the North, of old, for the comfort of the Mandarins, there had been the lumbering, two-wheeled, horse-drawn Peking cart. Now, here, manned sedan chairs and burden-bearing coolies still traversed the narrow stone-slab footpaths. Such were the simple and leisurely ways. The new day was calling for mechanized power and speed via highways and skyways.

Around us the quiet of the countryside began to be awakened by the clatter and shouts of highway construction, motor roads stretching out in four directions, all crudely built out of clay and chipped rock, all done by hand labor. What a sight and boon it was for isolated village folk to have a motor bus come by, opening to them broader areas of life. And no wonder our campus crowds, five miles out of the city, would pack sixty into a bus designed for twenty. The appeal of convenience and speed left comfort a small consideration. Grace and I ventured on a bus trip to Nanking: bumpy road, wide cracks in floor, hot day, two hundred miles; would we be recognizable? After one look, our hostess declared, "The kindest thing I can do is to offer you a bath."

Then came the construction of the great Chien Tang River bridge. For three successive years, before our eyes moved the spectacular developments of this amazing structure: the enormous cement caissons, the driving of the piles, rearing up of abutments, the double-decker steel rigging for railway and highway, and the final completing link of rails and pavement. There it stood as a monument to modernization. And appropriately enough, the nine-hundred-year-old towering pagoda on the edge of the bluff became linked in the landscape with the two-mile structure of cement and steel. Now the old and the new had merged.

Aviation also had joined the march, serving both civil and military purposes. Five miles east of the city rose the Central Aviation Training School. It offered great attraction for youth. These budding fliers enjoyed saluting our campus with roaring motors and low-gliding antics.

Likewise, the air waves were becoming popular avenues for communication, opening a new medium (in urban areas only) for news, education, and the gospel message. I recalled the thrilling occasion many years earlier when through clamped earphones I had heard strains of music from twenty miles away. Now the "wireless" had come to China. Out of this new marvel of radio transmission shortly arose the Christian Broadcasting Station in Shanghai, sponsored by a dedicated Christian businessman and operating twenty-four hours a day in several dialects.

Unfortunately, such an array of progressive achievements in the early thirties could not tell the whole story. Some frustrations plagued the National Government; some disillusions began to disturb the public. The most galling affront for the established Kuomintang to face and deal with was the insidious threat to national unity. There remained still an active rival in the land. The alarming fires of Chinese Communism, presumably extinguished in 1928, had continued to flare up here and there. In fact, as early as November, 1931, a Chinese-Soviet government established itself in the southwest province of Kiangsi, where it was entrenched in the countryside hills around Juichin. Dealing with this intolerable rebel establishment, Generalissimo Chiang Kai-shek applied his military might of army and air force in a series of bandit-suppression campaigns. But the assumed victories proved to be empty. The wily so-called bandits could not be crushed. In October, 1935, these irrepressible Communists began their "long march" (six thousand miles) into Shensi Province in the remote northwest, there to reestablish their capital in the caves of Yenan.

Another problem, not unrelated to the first, was exposing a serious shortcoming of the Kuomintang. What had the Government done for the peasantry? It appeared to rely on feeding them with paper promises. The urgency of relieving the generally exploited peasants must have been

realized, but the problem was found too difficult to handle
by an administration tied to business interests, where often merchants were also landlords. A mood of disappointment swept over the rural masses. When would they get
their land-tenure reform?

A third responsibility and commitment of the National
Government was the laying of the groundwork for modern
democracy in China. Actually, the Organic Law of the Republic of China (October 12, 1928) provided for one-party
dictatorship, the Kuomintang operating as an authoritarian
government and at the same time serving as an agency for
political training of the people. Having appropriated, as
general policy, Sun Yat-sen's Three Principles of the People, stressing the spirit of nationalism, individual rights
(democracy), and adequate livelihood, the Kuomintang
had also committed itself to Sun's "three stages of reconstruction": the completion of military unification, a period
of political training, and the setting up of constitutional
government.

Quite obviously, popular self-government in China could
be projected only as an aim to be realized some time in the
future. Would it require five, ten, or twenty years of Party
tutelage? One had to sense the magnitude of the task. In
terms of political science, both in theory and experience, a
stable democratic government rests upon certain basic requirements: general adult literacy, sense of citizenship,
concept of the rule of law, expression of public opinion,
extensive suffrage, a healthy party system with accepted
opposition, and a body of politically experienced governing personnel. In respect to most of these requirements
China had laid scarcely any foundations. Therefore, the
National Government was bound to operate bureaucrati-
cally, ruling from the top down; and since the Government
operated under a single party that cherished its power,

there also was the risk that the people's training would become a minor concern.

The Christian colleges did not fail to take up the new challenge. Surely the developing of citizenship consciousness and the providing of training for public functions should not be regarded as beyond academic concerns. Political science took on new dimensions. Youth, becoming politically minded (now along positive lines), brought to our department swelling classes and enlarged staff. Beyond the needs of those aspiring to a political career, was the need of each student, whatever his future vocation, to have an elemental knowledge of law and government.

How should one teach government and politics to Chinese students? The difference lay in traditions of East and West. Throughout the ages China had been governed by custom and usage, without written law, either constitutional or civil, and on the theory that the government governs best that governs least. As Lin Yu-tang (*My Country and My People,* 1935) was pointing out, Chinese youth found it difficult to be public-spirited in a society where legal protection was not given to personal rights. He asserted that the most striking characteristic of their political life as a nation was the absence of a constitution and the idea of civil rights. Yet, he also found merit in the fact that "a personal, human touch always colors the Chinese conception of law and government." So then, one could not help pondering, perhaps this concept helps to explain why the legalist philosophy of Han Fei-tsu in the third century B.C. never took hold and why the Chinese humanist culture proved so remarkably enduring. However, government by law is a modern necessity.

In our arrangement, my Chinese associates introduced for general knowledge the elements of law and offered a course in history of Chinese foreign relations, while I laid my stress upon comparative governmental systems. It appeared of prime importance that departmental students gain an understanding of the various systems as organized and operating in leading Western countries and how each was adapted to historical experience and national temperament. We noted in the U.S.A. strong presidential leadership attended with checks and balances, in France stress upon administrative stability due to many parties, in Great Britain a flexible and responsible parliament, and in Soviet Russia a single-party-directed socialism, each expressing its particular type of democracy.

Throughout these studies I did not deem it prudent (as a noncitizen) to attempt applications to the National Government. What I accented sharply was that democracy is not something to be bodily transplanted from one people to another. It is a treasure to be molded out of native soil. In a special message to the student body, I concluded thus: "The welfare of the Homeland is the welfare of each and it calls for a large measure of self-discipline and devotion. The responsible citizen will always bear in mind that there can be no true liberty without adequate authority and no peace and unity without compromise and cooperation. The house of Democracy will be long in the building and each of us is a bearer of lime and brick."

Already there loomed a crucial question: Would Nationalist China have a reasonable chance to develop her democratic processes? In the northeast there arose the alarming threat of Japan's advance into Manchuria. Could it portend a stroke at the heart of the Chinese nation? Across the land swept a wave of student patriotism. Students were determined to bolster up the Government for taking strong action against the invaders. On the campus an Anti-Japanese Patriotic Committee took form and hastily arranged for the whole student body to travel by train to Nanking with a petition for declaring war on Japan. They also proceeded to organize volunteer units and ask for military supplies. After a severe clash in Shanghai between Chinese and Japanese troops, tension reached new heights, so that in 1935 the Central Government arranged for the college to operate a Reserve Officers Training Corps, putting student dormitory living on a military basis. However, students were advised not to enter the ranks but to pursue their college studies.

In this threatening crisis a spirit of solidarity seemed to possess the country, and to many came the reassuring mood, Thank God for Chiang Kai-shek. Now China again had a leader, one such as had not arisen during the past century. Indeed, President Chiang, by displaying a genius for authority and public administration, had built among his countrymen a body of esteem, loyalty, and confidence, standing thus in the tradition of the strong man, devoted and able to serve the needs of the hour. Appraisal by those who knew him intimately credited him with qualities of resourcefulness, determination, political astuteness, and personal incorruptibility.

Quite naturally, Chiang Kai-shek paid frequent visits to Hangchow. Here special esteem awaited him, the favorite son of Chekiang Province. Also, as a place of restful retreat, the Generalissimo and the Madame maintained a lovely little villa at the edge of West Lake. Once, on the special occasion of our hosting the National Athletic Meet, the college enjoyed the honor of their presence among us in the college stadium.

In review, those buoyant years of constructive nationalism (1928–1936) looked good in achievement and in future promise. On the Hills several more new buildings had arisen, while student body and staff steadily expanded. Generally, a wide range of Christian institutions was thriving and increasing in influence. In public office and in private enterprise, Christian leaders exercised influence far beyond their numbers and, most significantly, the head of state had embraced the Bible faith.

Similarly, in our family affairs the years brought many happy experiences. The fresh mountain breezes along with rich water-buffalo milk nourished a pair of hardy little maidens who chattered Chinese with their devoted amah and went by ricksha (four miles) to the tiny American Primary School in the city, where mothers taught by turn. Summer vacations brought family reunions at the attractive north-coast resort of Tsingtao, where then Stanton and Sarah—plus Kathy and Bobby—were living. Furthermore, the year 1931 had brought us a very special guest, my younger brother, Earl, who voyaged via China on the way to a year in London on scholarship from the University of Toronto.

The early thirties being Depression years in the U.S.A., we on the outposts of service abroad were privileged to share the burdens of the home churches—a 10 percent cut in allowances and the period between furloughs extended to eight years. With the advantages of healthful location, our family managed to avoid any serious breakdown under the tensions of the time, although we became very weary. We had fortunately escaped the area's prevalent and ever-threatening malady. A visiting Mission secretary once dramatically proposed: "Live with a vim and die with a bang!"—to which Mother Mattox aptly fired back: "Have you ever heard of malaria?"

7

FACING REALITIES OF WAR

*A*UGUST 14, 1937, stands as a date of destiny. Our little family had just arrived in Seattle to board ship for return to China at the close of our second furlough—when came the flash! We were struck with the unbelievable news of bombs being dropped into the International Settlement of Shanghai. Such devastating madness could upset the whole pattern of international relations and with it our opportunities for regular missionary service. Could we even enter China if the great port city had become a theater of war? But, realizing that news reports tend to be spectacular and receiving no instructions to the contrary, we embarked with our two girls (ages nine and seven) and headed for the Asiatic coast.

About mid-ocean the awaited word came from New York by telegraph message. We received the advice: "Shanghai not accessible—wait in Japan or proceed to Manila." With this, we realized that Japan's aggressive designs and movement had reached the stage of open conflagration. It could mean nothing less than the bare fact of a real Sino-Japanese war, which would condition all manner of life and activities in both countries, probably for many years duration. Toward this we moved. And, as a time and place for reflection and appraisal, what could be better than our ship, that tiny floating island in the heart of the vast Pacific?

In the first place, contemplating the catastrophic effects of war between these two Asiatic neighbors became an almost unbearable thought. Fifteen years of identification with the people of China had borne its fruits, but I also cherished the rich memory of a goodwill tour in Japan. In the summer of 1931, I had participated in a tour of the country with a group of Chinese students. Through Christian auspices, especially the "Fellowship of Reconciliation," our group was afforded wide contacts and many courtesies toward understanding social and cultural aspects of Japanese society, and enjoyed the friendly spirit of the people. At the same time, our Chinese students seemed to leave a very favorable impression by their alertness and appreciativeness. Unhappily, this venture in goodwill, so enthusiastically initiated by my brother Stanton, fell short of its hopes. The following summer, when Japanese Christian students planned to reciprocate, they could not be offered a welcome to China, so embittered had the public become by Japan's aggressive actions in Manchuria.

Looking back, we recalled that Japan's hostilities against her neighbor had begun in September, 1931. Following the faked "Mukden railway incident," the militarists proceeded to bring all Manchuria under Japanese domain, making it nothing more than a puppet state. Then in July, 1937, a cleverly perpetrated clash near Peking was made the pretext and prelude to progressive military control of North China. While the National Government kept hesitating, inadequately prepared and still hoping for some negotiated solution, the early weeks of August had brought terror to the defenseless land. First, the port of Tientsin suffered dire destruction, and this was followed by considerable bombings of several large eastern cities, especially Nanking, Soochow, and Hangchow.

Brief daily news reports, as they reached us on board ship, offered little that was encouraging. In Shanghai, it seemed that a concentration of Japanese troops had begun landing on the northern edge, while at the same time, the leading battleship *Idzuma* moved up the Whangpoo directly in front of the International Settlement. Apparently this challenge was accepted as the expedient time and place for Chinese armed resistance. The whole world would immediately be awakened to the intolerable situation!

Later, to our surprise, we learned that the fateful bombs dropped upon the Settlement populace came mostly from Chinese planes. Several eager fliers had set out from the Hangchow Aviation Training School, bent on destroying the *Idzuma*. Harassed by Japanese fighter attacks and one of the fliers disabled by serious wounds, they missed their target; and the explosives had fallen upon highly congested areas.

This "Black Saturday" left its record of nearly two thousand killed and many more wounded. Among the multitude of casualties was the well-known Rev. Frank Rawlinson, editor of the *Chinese Recorder,* leading journal of Protestant missions in China. His tragic death, such a great loss to the missionary community, also marked the first foreign victim of the China-Japan War. However, the terrible disaster was accidental; and presumably the International Settlement was not intended to become involved in the theater of war. Nevertheless, the Chinese-controlled areas of the city suffered serious fighting and devastation.

Now, in 1937, we also vividly recalled the surging anti-Japanese feeling of the past few years. Throughout the entire country, students had been vigorously advocating the boycott of Japanese goods, educating the public by parades, banners, and slogans, and pleading with merchants to enforce restrictions. Incidentally, we ourselves got caught in this pressure. Inviting a graduating class into our home for a foreign-style dinner, we stumbled into a snag. The joyful chatter about Western customs, foods, and flavors suddenly ceased, as attention centered on what the salad dish of bright red jello was composed of. Alas, inquiry unearthed an ingredient of Japanese origin and both guests and hosts were equally dismayed. We made apology for our thoughtlessness and trusted we would be duly pardoned for having done this "evil thing."

Another related experience came out of my summer trip to Manchuria in 1935. This hot spot was known in international politics as the "tinderbox of Asia." Without difficulty my brother and I toured several areas and especially made a visit to the new capital, Hsinking (formerly called Changchun). We wished to observe for ourselves what conditions prevailed and what autonomies the people enjoyed. While Japanese mastery showed no great outward evidence, it was not difficult to see what a hoax lay behind the term "Manchukuo," implying an independent country. An intimate conversation with a Chinese friend, by title a high Government official, confirmed our impression sharply. With candor and shame, he declared, "We are nothing but oxen for the Japanese."

As time and events moved on, Chiang Kai-shek's continued reluctance to plunge into war became a puzzle and stumbling block to many. How does one calculate the burden of war or the price of freedom? In 1936, the generalissimo's policy of wait-and-see began to wear thin. Popular demands for armed resistance became more vocal, coming especially from students, including youth delegations to

Nanking. Still the official line held: not to forsake peace until there was no hope, and only in the last extremity should China make the sacrifice.

The Chinese had a long tradition of being a peace-loving people. Did it not seem better to build a wall for protection, or to compromise if you must, as a maneuver for survival? Clearly, China was technically ill-prepared to meet a foe so industrially advanced, having had barely a decade to achieve unity and strength under the National Government. And then, there were also hopes in the peace-making machinery of the League of Nations, possible mediation by Western powers, and the mighty weight of world opinion. Would these be of no avail in China's critical hour?

Beyond all this, the sharpest thorn in Chiang Kai-shek's flesh was the rival Chinese Communist government within the land. The situation became to him a veritable nightmare. Five years of persistent suppression, and still no unified China! Without first crushing the foe within, how could the country stand solidly against a foreign power? At the same time, Japan kept justifying her actions on grounds of the Communist threat, proclaiming it her mission "to liberate China and lay the foundation for peace in East Asia."

However, during 1936, public pressures welled up against the halting Government. The so-called National Salvation unions, representing professors, students, and labor, en masse advocated national unity in opposing Japanese aggression. By clear implication, this amounted to a call for the Government to abandon its anti-Communist campaigns. Then, late in December when we were furloughing in Toronto, Canada, startling headline news swept the world: "Kidnapping of the President of China!" Having proceeded to the northwest to inspect the progress

of his "Communist Suppression Army" (under the Man-
churian General Chang Hsueh-liang), the generalissimo
had been seized and forcibly detained by his own officers.
Nanking, aghast at such a turn of events, rocked with confusion and perplexity. With this dramatic "Sian incident,"
in which Chiang Kai-shek's life appeared to be at stake,
came the turning point of Nationalist policy. Chiang con-
sented to abandon civil strife and seek a working agreement for a united front against Japan.

Such appeared to be the background of policies and
events preceding the clash of open war, with all its involvements, into which we were about to step as we sailed
across the Pacific.

The S.S. *President Grant* docked in Yokohama, August
27. Approaching this hour of decision, over eighty China-
bound missionaries had been counseling in huddles as to
what to do next. Those destined for still-open South China
would quite naturally be proceeding to Hong Kong, but
for us (and Mr. and Mrs. Van Evera), stopping in Japan
seemed the best choice. Surely a way would be opened to
enter China. Almost immediately we learned that American authorities, in the interests of safety, had set a complete ban on nationals entering China at whatever point.
While, in our case, British passports allowed broader liberties, we did have grave concern for our children. Presently, confirming word reached us from other Hangchow
missionaries detained in Japan after summer vacation that
our China Council instructed us all to remain there for the
time.

By courtesy of our fellow Presbyterian workers in Japan,
arrangements were made for a couple of weeks' stay at the
noted Karaizawa Mountain Resort. This entirely unexpected experience, offering so much beauty, comfort, and
friendliness, was then followed by a month of refugeeing

within the throbbing life of Tokyo. Here we encountered the military spirit in the country that was the enemy to our China. A revealing experience it proved to be.

In a manner of speaking, we felt a mutual embarrassment in this close association between China and Japan missionaries, with our respective countries in the grip of war. To our relief, we found that these friends not only shared our distress but also were bearing the burden of Japan's rampant militarism. Our location made us the more vulnerable. Day and night the cheers for departing soldiers at the nearby railway station pained our hearts. Alas, these young men were being sent on the noble mission of "saving China" and glorifying the Land of the Rising Sun. From a missionary long serving in Japan came this prophetic statement: "This will not be over until every home in Japan has a bereavement, and many a person will find that he has a key but no house."

Among our many appreciated contacts was acquaintance with the Karl Reischauer family. Esteemed founder and president of the Tokyo Girls' School, he was then heading the Presbyterian Mission, and it was one of his sons who died in the Shanghai bombing. We also had the pleasure of visiting Miss Alma Kaufman (from my hometown—Kitchener, Ontario), who was secretary of the International Y.W.C.A. and many years resident in Tokyo. How good it was to see again the noted social worker and evangelist Toyohiko Kagawa, once a guest in our home when attending a church conference on the Hangchow campus. For a brief interview, I enjoyed the gracious presence of the head of the Church of Christ in Japan. With necessary reserve and caution, he shared some deep concerns for the faith and for the nation. It was no secret that police surveillance required daily report on whom he talked with and about what matters.

These contacts and many others left a rich store of understanding and fellowship arising from those restless weeks of our Tokyo interlude. As the war crisis deepened, a group of distressed Christian leaders kept meeting in penitence and prayer. Perhaps the most precious expression of all, representing the burdened spirit of Japanese Christians, came from a direct report by one of our missionary friends. Kagawa, he said, was literally stricken to the earth in grief. This saintly man unveiled his broken spirit in these words: "I have no heart for anything. I am not alive; the real Kagawa died in Peiping some months ago. I would like to be on my face before the Chinese people, doing penance for the sins of my country. But I cannot do that; I am unable."

Finally we could enter the port of Shanghai! Fires of war's devastation still glowed upon the horizon as we approached the city by a French steamship late in October. The International Settlement, in which the docks are located, however, appeared fairly normal. The first urgency for us was to attend to the girls' schooling. We had them entered into the well-favored Shanghai American School, where emergency lodging was found in the dormitory for all of us.

How good to be back in China again! Perhaps no place could better symbolize law, order, and freedom than this quiet residential area in the French Concession. Together, the Settlement and Concession remained a precious island of security, while in the Chinese City all around, there prevailed the severities of enemy occupation. On the north side, the Honkew section was harboring a large contingent of the Japanese army; but the area to the south, more strictly the Chinese City, presented on its face the shambles of war.

What had become of our Presbyterian compound at the

South Gate? We were taken out to see. Fortunately, the boys' school, girls' school, and church buildings had escaped serious damage, with only a few residences demolished. Some distance away, on a teeming Chinese thoroughfare, stood the Nantao Christian Institute building practically unscathed. What a remarkable sight! With rubble all around, this ministering social-service center loomed up to symbolize the Protecting Hand in the midst of human disaster.

Clearly the most pathetic aspect of Shanghai was its forlorn mass of refugees. In the city of three million, one fourth of them had been bombed out, burned out, or otherwise displaced; and all were totally destitute. Most of these had been congregated into refugee camps, being dependent exclusively on public charity. The Red Cross, Salvation Army, and other benevolent agencies administered no less than 175 improvised camps for these homeless and helpless. Quite close to us, occupying a vacated campus, milled a mass of fifteen thousand, presumably fairly well administered; but the most wretched camp we visited offered only flimsy shelter and hopelessly inadequate provision of food. To help relieve this plight, our group sent over on Thanksgiving Day a store of vegetables to liven up their rations of boiled water and a bit of meal.

From a land of abundance in America and a land of military madness in Japan, we had now plunged into China's heart of misery. Yet it seemed to us that we had come home, where we ought to be. Here it was where we could "sing the Lord's song" by sharing the burdens and distresses of the people to whom we were sent.

My objective, of course, was Hangchow. There was word of the college in operation and the urgent need for my arrival; but the matter of travel presented no simple situation. Normally an express train could reach Hangchow

in four hours. However, the Japanese army, holding a portion of this direct railway line, left only one possible route
—a coastal steamer to Ningpo and then across country by
a perilous night train frequently subjected to bombings.
Both Chinese and foreigners kept seeping out this way,
but hardly anyone was going in.

Nightfall at the Ningpo station found two Baptist missionaries and me getting settled in a rickety and unlighted
railway coach. We huddled into our blankets against the
December winds coming through shattered windows, and
the train began creeping along for a twelve-hour journey
through the unknown. Finally, as the welcome morrow
dawned, we realized ourselves gliding peacefully across
the great Chien Tang River bridge, safe and elated to be
back in Hangchow. This bridge afforded a full panoramic
view of the college grounds. And now—what secrets were
hidden beneath this manifest beauty that draped the
Dragon Hills?

Immediately on stepping out at the suburban station, I
sensed around me a strange world, all so awesomely quiet.
Inhabitants, there were none! On that morning of December 6, 1937, I mounted the winding campus path only to
discover another emptiness. Only Dr. Robert McMullen,
senior missionary, held fort, assisted by a few Chinese
aides and several servants. I was told that they had tried
to reach me in Tokyo by letter and telegram (none of
which I had received) in order to hasten my coming. Now
my arrival was too late for joining the southwest move of
five hundred students and staff members fleeing the war!
Apparently I had missed my great opportunity to be where
I was most needed.

8

IN THE GRIP OF CONQUEST

*A*CTUALLY the college had been carrying on for some months before December, 1937, under nerve-straining harassments, always on alert for siren warnings. Dugouts and shelters were put to use against strafings and bombings. As protection to foreign-owned property, there lay spread out on the quadrangle an American flag of such impressive proportions (40 by 60 feet) that no approaching plane could miss seeing it. When suddenly the Chinese defense line crumbled under overwhelming air bombardment some miles up the railway, it seemed the hour had struck for a break. On the basis of rumors of imminent danger, apparently the campus had been hit by panic, the excitement and confusion of which I could well imagine. And yet, should not I have been one of that motley mass in hasty flight by rowboat or trudging along the road at the hour of midnight?

I was told about the bombings over the city. Remarkably, the effects were not so serious after all, actually with no loss of life, though the railway station appeared a mere shell after repeated strikes. However, Hangchow had already involved herself deeply in the war by providing refuge for the wounded. The terrific losses in the Kashing battle (midway to Shanghai) and the frightful bombing and strafing of trains and depots along the railway were flooding hospitals and homes with fully ten thousand disabled men.

Very little evidence could be observed locally of the Chinese armed defense, inconspicuously billeted in secluded monastery and temple grounds and other unsuspected buildings. The fighting spirit was rated high. Japanese inhumanity in Shanghai battles, where surrendered soldiers and truckloads of wounded were ruthlessly machine-gunned, had roused the fires of hatred. Sadly, however, against such unrelenting air bombardment the Chinese had no real defense.

That strange sense of emptiness which struck me upon arrival kept creeping progressively through shop and home across the entire city, as a panic-stricken populace was taking flight. On the shock of the Japanese breakthrough, Hangchow was emptied by at least a hundred thousand within a few days. By every possible means they fled, multitudes walking hundreds of miles, seeking the safety of western Anhwei. Foreign residents faced a like situation. Of the missionaries, only twenty-five remained at their posts, all women with children having been sent out. Chinese pastors had a crucial decision to make: whether to lead the major portion of their flock, moving off to Free China, or to share with those remaining the burdens of enemy occupation.

Upon reflection, I could not feel that the character of the college and its continuing service were critically threatened by our vacant campus. In its pervading Christian spirit lay our assurance and hope. Particularly was this maturity of the faith manifested in the life of our devoted president, Baen Lee. I was told that at the last staff prayer meeting, he fervently prayed for the Japanese and implored that the Chinese be kept from bitterness of heart, and in sobs he closed his prayer with: "Father, forgive them, for they know not what they do."

Now, at this crucial stage of fighting, all of us could see the fall of Hangchow as inevitable and imminent. And the burden of it, weighing so grievously upon the responsible civic leaders, was challenging them to courage. Surely, a way could be found to provide a measure of relief and safety. How? First, of the ten thousand wounded soldiers, about one tenth lay in too critical condition to be evacuated. Again, how could the multitude of helpless women and children be provided with places of refuge?

Hope was born out of Christian concern and prayer. Mr. Chu Kung-yang, Hangchow Y.M.C.A. secretary, was first to grasp an idea. By his urging, a consultative group composed of several Chinese from the Chamber of Commerce and Public Health agencies, along with leaders of the various missions, assembled quietly in the Mission Hospital compound. Bound together in purpose and inspired by the trustful prayer of Bishop Deymier (French Roman Catholic), this group laid their plans for dealing with these pressing human needs.

An International Relief Association took form and a local branch of the Red Cross was set up. Four nationalities formed the leadership: American, British, French, and Chinese—with Rev. R. J. McMullen serving as chairman and Dr. S. D. Sturton as secretary. As never before, Protestants, Catholics, and Buddhists began to labor together in complete accord for the urgent relief of humanity; and first, by a venture of faith, all the most critically wounded soldiers were harbored in the British hospital in hope of safety under a neutral flag.

Then the question of sanctuary for refugees, particularly the women and children, brought forth a daring con-

cept. Why not appeal to save the entire city by proposing
to both armies that Hangchow be peacefully occupied by
the Japanese, with a guarantee of no defense by the Chinese in return for the safety of its occupants and property?
When the terrifying news struck us of the armed atrocities
committed against Chinese civilians in Nanking and of the
wanton destruction of Soochow, efforts were intensified to
have our city spared. Through the Red Cross, a plea was
dispatched to the Chinese army. Then, by way of the
American, British, and French consulates, the request was
laid before the Japanese high command.

To our great relief, this desperate hope of sparing Hangchow by having the city declared an unfortified zone,
proved an acceptable arrangement to both armies. Nevertheless, as a reasonable safeguard against the contingency
of several days' disorder during the turnover to the Japanese, several Red Cross camps were laid out and provisioned for an estimated four thousand to five thousand
refugees.

Around mid-December it was considered that about one-
half million people had departed from Hangchow. With
another hundred thousand then taking flight before the arrival of the Japanese army, the population had dropped to
about one fourth of its original. Most of those remaining to
face the ordeal belonged to the lowest economic level; and
it is to be noted that practically all of these spoke pure
Hangchow dialect, proving that they had truly belonged
to this place for generations.

On the afternoon of December 22, Dr. McMullen and I
went into the city for a Red Cross meeting at which he was
presiding. There a member of the municipal government
quietly passed the word around that the time had arrived,
and that tomorrow Hangchow would be occupied by the
Japanese army. He advised foreigners of a last train going

out that evening in case any wished to leave by rail across the river. As to the two of us, residing on the college campus quite outside the safety zone, he urged that we remain in the city for several days. This we declined. We had resolved to see it through on the campus, which was American property and presumably safe, though very exposed to the Chinese defenses set up across the river.

The major portion of the Chinese army had already withdrawn to the opposite side of the Chien Tang River, while a section moved just beyond the western outskirts of the city. As to the police force, they also marched away in regular formation past our campus, toward the town of Fuyang, twenty miles southwest. No provincial or municipal officials remained within the city. The Chamber of Commerce took charge.

All seemed quiet that evening, except for the sounds of the still-fleeing people streaming steadily across the bridge. Having kept in telephone contact with Hangchow until midnight, we turned to our rest, though uneasily. Three hours later, I felt myself sharply lifted from my bed by a terrific boom. Reaching for the light switch, I found it was dead. So! The splendid modern power plant, about two miles away and edging the city, had been blasted as an act of sabotage by the retreating Chinese. The "scorched earth" policy had begun.

Now came the question of the magnificent new bridge. Would this splendid double-decker structure, fruit of three years' feverish labor, pride of engineers and population alike, become also a sacrifice to the god of war? It had been rumored that the bridge must go. The Chinese command would most probably adopt this strategy for cutting the enemy's southwest advance.

What a beautiful day had burst upon our lonely Hill! Red roses blooming, birds softly chirping, no sound of falling bombs; only the unceasing flow of rickshas, handcarts, and wheelbarrows trailing behind their owners as they crossed the spanning bridge. In this paradoxical mood of quiet apprehension, we kept an alert watch from our campus front, only five minutes' walk from the bridgehead. At midafternoon, I observed the traffic cease and the bridge being cleared of people. Then, as if struck by a giant hand, the entire structure appeared to stagger, with four of the eighteen spans slumping zigzag into the river. Moments later came the thunderous shock that quaked our buildings and sent echoes across the hills. In effect, this act established the Chinese resistance on the opposite bank and put our campus into a no-man's-land.

In the meantime, the Japanese Imperial Army was making without obstruction its triumphal occupation of the "open city." Despite the appalling experience and not without misgivings, there prevailed a general mood of gratitude and relief that Hangchow was being spared. Immediately foreign residents were provided with guarantees for safety of life and property. However, we shortly began to realize how a city laden with affluence and cultural treasure becomes a wide-open harvest to a hundred thousand troops fresh from the heat of battle.

"The Japanese soldiers are the most civilized in the world." So it was confidently stated by the high command, leaving us to question by what standards they measured and what they regarded as the necessities of war. Depredations may be a matter of degree with any occupying army. In this case, it just seemed taken for granted that all things should lend themselves freely to the needs, the conveniences, and often to the whims and lusts of the invader. Presently Hangchow fell into a state of hopeless disorder. Shops and houses were systematically broken into and plundered. The bewildered people, frightfully harassed, many robbed of necessary personal belongings, also fell victim to the shameful violence commonly imposed upon women.

In less than a week, fully ten thousand women and children had taken refuge in the Red Cross shelters. Here alone were safety, seclusion, and food. It seemed, after all, ours was a conquered city; or should we recognize that the Japanese had special problems of army discipline? At the height of this reign of terror, the Red Cross was harboring seventeen thousand and the Buddhist Red Swastika Society another eight thousand. Included in this number were many brought in from surrounding villages where battles had been raging. Ultimately, these special sanctuaries, located in mission compounds, the Y.M.C.A., and a Buddhist temple, became an embarrassment to responsible Japanese authorities. They wanted them disassembled. But they could not give guarantee to the guardians of the sanctuaries for the safety of these people should they be dispersed outside.

Generally, my personal responsibilities kept me on the campus. The exacting requirements of safeguarding our exposed and unwalled Mission property and caring for our small isolated community offered little chance for going into the city. But, after a week of "peaceful occupation," I did go and was presented with a shocking and despairing sight. On the once-elegant Great Street, the main business section, every shop had been thoroughly ransacked. A peep into a drugstore, for example, revealed utter confusion of discarded items over counter and floor, while shelves, benches, and stools were broken up for fuel. Another area of small shops had been turned into a stabling place for the army animal transport. And where did that horse get his silk-padded quilt? Everywhere prevailed oppression and misery.

A more intimate view of the tragic happenings came to me from our Baptist co-worker, E. H. (Ed) Clayton, in charge of the Wayland Academy Refuge Center. From the three-hundred-person capacity, which they had reached on the first day, they soon found themselves sheltering five times that number. Dawn of the second day brought a desperate clamoring at the gate. Thirty-nine women and girls stood there begging to be received and not one of them had escaped rape.

Nothing could be done for the men between ages of sixteen and sixty. It might evoke suspicion of harboring spies. The constant demand of the enemy for able-bodied carriers left small choice and slight mercy for them. One had a choice of a fifty-mile trip or a bayonet thrust. For a man to try to protect the honor of his home and family meant to risk his life. A neighbor and his wife, protesting assault, both died on the spot! A few small boys on the street, staring at a soldier leading a donkey laden high with loot, were given a rifle charge! Who could feel safe from violent death?

As earlier mentioned, the military situation was now placing our campus squarely on the battlefront. Paradoxically enough, we were within the Japanese territory and subjected to Chinese rifle fire from across the river. Every moving object on our side presented a target. The Nipponese commander was concerned out of respect for our neutrality and sharply advised us to withdraw. "We cannot be responsible for your safety," he urged. In the interests of the Mission property and the welfare of the local Chinese there, we resolutely decided to stay.

Actually, we could keep reasonably well sheltered behind our collection of substantial buildings and well-wooded grounds. However, Mack's Red Cross duties in the city meant his passing over a half-mile section of exposed riverside road—a real hazard! On those occasional daring trips by the college car, our faithful Chinese driver, Swang Hsi, had both the right and the need to brag about courage. While his passenger could slump low in the rear, he merely trusted to the dubious reliability of a silk-padded quilt spread over the old soft-topped Ford, and he stepped on the gas!

Expediency determined that between ourselves and the Japanese we maintain a policy of respectful relations. While claiming our right as neutrals, we realized our almost total dependency upon the goodwill of army officials. We could note a distinct shade of animosity toward the British, undoubtedly in anticipation of the inevitable clash with British interests in East Asia. However, they apparently did not expect conflict with America, and fortunately, these officials showed us a cooperative mood. They were careful to post sealed army notices for the protection of our campus buildings, provided us with a special guard, and urged that we report any difficulties. This situation and arrangement made possible our continuing services. While for us it was perilous and odious, with them it also required considerable forbearance. We were grateful for the mutual spirit of accommodation, integrity, and faith.

Our brick house on the hillside, though clearly exposed, was well shuttered, and we added blankets over windows at dusk to ensure blackout conditions. Then no one ventured out, not even the Japanese guard. The Chinese guerrillas had the run of things at night! Each day I inspected the brush-covered ravines to see that no one was hiding there; and when one morning I spied a dagger under a bit of straw in the flower bed, it was promptly handed over to the guard. Almost daily our buildings caught a spray of Chinese bullets. Yet in good providence, no one in our little community was hit by these.

Then came our New Year's Day "campus battle," as we called it. Suddenly an intense attack of rifle fire struck our grounds. It was directed against a group of Japanese soldiers who for safety had left the open road and dispersed on our wooded hillside. Bullets whizzed overhead and ripped through hedges as we dashed for shelter, then small artillery opened action in both directions. After the skirmish and general excitement, all quieted down and the crisis seemed over. Then tragedy hit us just at dusk. A rifle cracked nearby and we heard a moan behind the hedge. Our faithful servant had been felled by a mortal shot. This poor inoffensive man had a bamboo carrying-pole in his hand, and in the evening shadows, it had made him appear like an armed guerrilla. The Japanese guard had killed him, a mistake for which the officer in charge expressed his regret.

Several weeks later, we found ourselves just on the edge of an all-day engagement being fought on our side of the river bend, where Chinese defense still held. The area suffered hours of heavy shelling and extensive fires. Our friend, young farmer Chu from the village behind the mountain, took the risk of bringing us food supplies the following dawn and related this appalling news. A score of villages were burned to the ground, he said; and he told of horrible atrocities. The fleeing villagers were rounded up; and 150 men, separated out as suspected soldiers in plain clothes, were mown down by machine guns. Later, from the temple on the hilltop, the Buddhist priest led two thousand refugees into the city to seek safety.

Our friend told about his own village. They were constantly being harassed and plundered, with here a woman outraged and there a man killed. They had had warning that soldiers were approaching, and the women hid among the hillside bushes. But not all had escaped. The farmer's pregnant young wife, crouching for hours in a culvert one day, had suffered too much exposure and later died of pneumonia. He asked in despair, "How long must we endure this?" My reply could offer little consolation. "It may be five years." Drawing his hand in a gesture across his throat, the farmer answered: "No! One year is enough. By that time we will all be dead."

A page of my diary, dated March 10, 1938, records: "Today I go out again to bury the fallen, the hapless dead. With me are a couple of servants, taking pick and shovel, rope and board, and accompanied by the Japanese guard. Yesterday there were eight, before five, and today a few more—all Chinese in civilian garb—youth, prime, and age. Perhaps the five behind the ridge, all stout fellows, hands bound and chests riddled, were soldiers in plain clothes. In the closest available spot we hastily bury them—away from the sight of man and the teeth of famished dogs. All are unknown graves of unknown Chinese civilians. When bullets whiz, we dodge behind a wall."

Into our reception room stepped a stocky young sergeant equipped with pistol and sword and a confident air. He spoke English. We sat down together with guards close by. "Respected teacher," he began, "how long do you think this war will last?" "I am a man of peace," I replied. "My heart is sad to see the Japanese army in China. No doubt the war will stop when your army returns home." A quick flash crosses his eyes. "But we had to come to fight the Communists and Chiang Kai-shek who has now joined them." "No," I said gently, "Chiang has always been against the Communists and still is." With a puzzled look, he bowed farewell and strode off.

We discovered that many common soldiers and officers had no taste for war. Having been called up for only a few months, they were still shopkeepers, dentists, or teachers, yearning to be back to family and occupations. Obviously some felt themselves victims of the "war machine"; others came to us definitely seeking Christian fellowship. "War is sinful," these said to us. "We want your prayers." Could it be providential that the lieutenant assigned to our district was a man of such faith and quality of spirit? When suddenly transferred, he quickly dispatched a bearer with a message of assurance that his successor would take care of us.

We did have some nasty situations. That our campus had been declared out of bounds did not prevent unruly soldiers from molesting women on the grounds or my coming face-to-face with unfriendly scowls and set bayonets. Once I heard a disturbance in the bamboo grove and found the very incongruous sight of a sublieutenant slashing fiercely at the stocks with his bayonet. "Ha," he said when he saw me, "see how strong I am?" Then, throwing down the weapon, he added, "But don't you see that I'm no good?" When he tried to hand me his pistol with the challenge to take it and shoot him, it seemed discreet for me to back off quickly and disappear . . . before he changed his mind as to who should be shot.

To us, the godsend of all the Japanese we had to deal with in the Hangchow area was Sergeant Fugimaru, staunch head of the military police. Relentlessly he battled disorder and abuse, rescuing the innocent and helpless, and often administering discipline on the spot. In Dr. Sturton's daily round of inspection of all the Red Cross camps, Sergeant Fujimaru was always in attendance and supplying encouragement. Although each foreign compound flew its own flag, had army proclamations posted at its gate, and was provisioned with stationed guards, this afforded only relative security. In numerous instances, when the

Red Cross called him from anywhere in the city, this dutiful man came almost immediately; the offender's face was soundly slapped, or he was hauled away to the military police station.

On one occasion, I caught a soldier making off with our electric fan. When he refused to yield it, I made a sharp mental note of his description and a protest was sent to the local commandant. Surprisingly, several days later, along came our trusty Fujimaru accompanied by a private carrying a fan. Following my identification of the culprit, he received a sharp reprimand and was required to bow in apology. Who would think that this could happen in the Japanese army? One can be sure that out of the grim ordeal of Hangchow's early months of occupation, Sergeant Fugimaru will be gratefully remembered for his acts of mercy and his quality of honor. He had been a police officer in his hometown of Kobe and had received his education in a mission school.

As the months passed, although a puppet self-government had been set up for the city, disorders and oppressions continued. In the outlying suburbs there was constant outbreak of gunfire as well as the harassment by Chinese guerrillas and snipers. Especially in the area adjoining our grounds, the raging flames of burning homes and fields made an appalling sight, which, we later heard, gave rise to the rumor in Shanghai that the whole college establishment was burning down.

It began to appear to us that the war had stalemated on the Hangchow front. In spite of repeated Japanese shellings, the Chinese contingent on the south side of the river could not be dislodged, nor did they really rout the Chinese forces on our side, still only five miles away. Scorched-earth tactics became so effective, with bridges blasted, railways torn up, and highways cut, that from day to day one could hardly be sure who might be holding Hangchow.

By the end of January, it became possible to send a letter to my family in Shanghai. This, of course, was restricted to unsealed material and dispatched by courtesy of the Imperial Army. A reply was also permitted. In mid-April, they granted me a two-week leave to Shanghai for X-ray treatment of my neuritis. Finally, in July, I was replaced by another Mission worker so that I might join the staff of the college, which had moved again. After disbanding at its interior location, it had reopened in the International Settlement in Shanghai.

What does it mean to be a pilgrim missionary, enmeshed in a war? We came to see that the essentials of Christian love and duty pointed to several tasks: that of being a watchman and policeman, protecting Mission property; that of serving as a relief worker, providing shelter and food for the dispossessed; that of standing as a buffer between helpless people and harsh soldiery. It seemed good to the Holy Spirit and to us (Acts 15:28) to give daily expression to faith, courage, and love in these situations of extremity. Giving witness to Christ in the most existential manner, more by deed than by word, seemed to become the light of Truth and the acceptable Way. In our campus-village group, Sunday preaching and weekly Bible study were always maintained. Almost everywhere, one could sense the awakening response to the good news. Especially was this so among the thousands in the refugee camps where the Word was made alive in demonstration and proclamation. As the poor heard the gospel, not a few were received by baptism into the faith.

9

INTERNATIONAL REFUGE

*J*ULY, 1938, carried me over into a new era. How refreshing it was to have the family circle restored and to be breathing again the free air of an international community.

Shanghai had its way of making adjustments and settling down to ride the storm, graciously affording a haven to the congregated millions. Despite the tenuous situation, the Settlement and Concession continued to remain as an island of peace within a surging sea of war. Here, as contrasted with the deteriorations of Hangchow, society had not been shattered at its base or robbed of its integrity. Here one could still feel the assuring sense of order and freedom, so essential to personal initiative and buoyancy. Here, also, lay open abounding opportunities for the exercise of our spiritual calling through Christian education and dynamic church life.

As always, this cosmopolitan center of the Orient presented the face of a great organism composed of many elements. Is it possible to behold the visage and gauge the spirit of so unique a world city in such a time? Can one measurably enter into its lights and shadows and follow sensitively the flow of events throughout these crucial four years? Here, in the midst of this international complex,

with its throbbing seaport, thriving commerce, political involvements, social glamour, humanitarian problems, intellectual pursuits and spiritual aspirations one could feel a
breadth of involvement and a fullness of living. One could
also see the ominous gathering of ever-darkening clouds,
foreboding worldwide disaster.

Hangchow College, after the abortive attempt to remain
in Free China by quickly fleeing westward, as the more
northern institutions (Yenching University, Peiping, Cheeloo University, Tsinan, and the University of Nanking)
had proceeded to do, found ready sanctum in Shanghai.
This was the natural place for the East-Central educational group. The great city teemed with eager youth, who
knew well that it was not the policy of the National Government for students to enter the armies but rather to pursue diligently their studies. Surely, their knowledge and
skills would be in urgent need for postwar reconstruction
and developments. For that reason Shanghai was becoming the one gathering place for the coastal provinces,
drawing its multitudes in search of learning.

It seemed, for the mission colleges of East China that
the hour had come for a significant forward step by achieving maximum service through combined effort. Promptly,
our denominational institutions linked hands. By this
union they constituted themselves as The Associated
Christian Colleges in Shanghai, composed of four institutions: St. John's University (Episcopal) and University of
Shanghai (Baptist), both of which had moved in from the
war-torn outskirts of the city, Soochow University (Methodist), and Hangchow College (Presbyterian). Hereby an
earlier projected dream for federation appeared to be
moving toward reality.

Consequently, the autumn of 1938 found both Grace and
me eager participants in that throbbing educational enter-

prise that, strangely enough, was situated in the heart of the business section on Nanking Road not far from the Bund. The spacious second floor of the well-known Continental Emporium Building, in affording classroom and administrative facilities for our nearly three thousand students, became a veritable beehive, daily in swarming.

For three fruitful years this cooperative mission venture continued steadily to thrive and expand. By arrangement, Hangchow College (hereafter called University) made its major academic contribution through the departments of commerce and engineering. These studies were rising to high priority in demand; but disciplines in the arts, such as linguistics, politics, and Christian ethics, followed close in student interest and pursuit.

Probably our richest and most outstanding service flowed from the newly established Hangchow University Church. Its ministry, designed to make real and relevant the light of the gospel, with its comfort and its challenge, touched the responsive chord of awakened spiritual need. From the small beginning of a Sunday morning gathering in the largest classroom, it expanded to the popularly attended worship service at the Roxy Theatre, averaging 750 earnest seekers and including many from Shanghai professional and business life. Into a multitude of hearts entered a freshness of faith and sustaining strength. Also, from the regular Bible study groups and special inquirer's classes came scores expressing commitment to Christ and seeking the fellowship of the church through the rite of Baptism.

For joyous spiritual expression, no doubt most inspiring and memorable were the festival services for Christmas and Easter, the high point being reached in the great oratorios, rendered by a sixty-voice choir, under the directorship of the National Conservatory of Music.

While Shanghai had its reputation for much shady "high

life" and glamorous amusement, hardly could it be said to
be ill-stocked with churches. Take the word of Carol All-
cott, our popular American radio commentator: "Remember! Shanghai has as many churches as nightclubs, and
they are just as active." Among the considerable number
and variety of churches (at least two hundred), Hangchow University Church conceived its special mission and
challenge to be the minds and hearts of youth.

Unfortunately, our makeshift educational setup was
bound to entail many inescapable restrictions and burdens.
Both academically and socially, little means for student
development could be provided beyond the mere conducting of classes and limited experiments. The whole range
of extracurricular functions stood practically blank.
Whence spring the fires of *esprit de corps* without accommodations for congregated residence, organized athletics,
and common social gatherings? Many depressives gave
urgent call for morale-building. With scattered families,
excessively crowded living conditions, and generally inadequate diet, inevitably both students and teachers were
suffering impairment of health and reduced mental efficiency.

Apart from the church service each Sunday at the Roxy,
our only means and times for collective gathering came
with the annual joint graduation exercises in the spacious
Grand Theater. How could we meet this pressing need for
something decidedly social—something really intimate and
creative and bolstering? So then, again, an intensive network of lively fellowship groups became the answer. Distributed by areas for convenient attendance and shared by
faculty members, these hearty fellowships afforded refreshing social intercourse, a spirit of comradeship, and a
welcome supplement of nourishing food and delicacies.

Our family life, with residence in a quiet area of the

French Concession, also took on a Shanghai normalcy, including among other things several readjustments due to housing shortage. An hour's trip on tram or bus carried us to our teaching work and, as to the girls, excellent schooling remained conveniently available in the Shanghai American School. Close by, also, were the facilities for religious instruction and the fellowship afforded by the American Community Church.

Particularly impressive to me was the freedom of getting around. This applied to most areas of Greater Shanghai and even beyond, requiring no more than a respectful bow to Japanese guards. Very surprisingly, in the spring of 1940, while there was an apparent lull in the fighting, we were able to obtain passes to Hangchow for the family. For a few cherished days we lived again on the familiar campus—still unscathed and gorgeously beautiful. The girls, reveling once more in their childhood haunts, roamed the hillsides and gathered armloads of pink azaleas while we packed up some household effects for use in Shanghai. For a moment it seemed one could forget the war—except for the distant rumbling and the terrible blight hanging heavily over the ravished land.

That summer, then, by special leave of the Mission, I made a speedy trip to Canada and back. Our previous term on the field had been such a long one, by the extension to eight years, thus making it a weary wait for my aging parents. On this account I promised my father and mother a special interim visit. The peaceful round-trip voyage on the Japanese liner and a full month at home meant a refreshing experience for me and a great comfort to my parents, who had been carrying a heavy burden of concern. We could thereafter look more calmly at life's uncertainties. Conversely, however, totally unknown to me, Grace and the girls had encountered a terrible ordeal in a small

Japanese coastal ship. Proceeding to the Tsingtao summer
resort, on medical advice, they were caught in the grip of a
severe typhoon and floundered helplessly for hours.

Then, to our distress, just a few months later came the
stunning family shock. Shanghai was no longer considered
safe! Everything began to point to an impending crisis between the United States and Japan. In case of military
emergency women and children must all be out. On this
situation and policy governments and missions were
agreed. Although we lingered on to the last in the process
of withdrawal, finally it swept us along. On the 26th of
December, 1940, as the tender putted away from the
Bund, we waved the final good-by. They were sailing on
the *Empress of Asia* to Vancouver, setting the vast ocean
between us—this at a time when any precipitous move
might trip down the curtain.

This time our family disruption struck a telling blow, requiring in both directions considerable emotional adjust-
ment. On my part, I plunged into intensive work. Only
redoubled efforts in teaching and student activities, it
seemed, could compensate for the loss and emptiness.
Again unanchored, I packed and shipped off a case of
freight, moved household effects to the Mission compound, and linked up with two men equally lonesome.
After all, we deemed the hardship of broken families as
yet a small sacrifice in a world so broken and full of suffering. We dubbed ourselves "The Owl Club" (AWL): Hille
Arthur, of Associated Missions Treasurers, Edwin Walline,
head of our Mission Council, and me, Lautenschlager—a
corporation not limited but quite indefinite. Number 16,
Route Winling, French Concession, became a sort of establishment.

An event of family significance occurred early in May. It
was one of those infrequent contacts with Stanton, who,

with Sarah, Kathy, and Bobby, was heading for a furlough. They had all come from Chengtu (West China) to Hong Kong by plane, and their ocean liner was now stopping a day in our port. I took Stanton to the Navy Y Tiffin Club, and in the evening we all had dinner together at the well-favored Chocolate Shop on Nanking Road. But the visit was brief. Carrying with them personal greetings and letters to my beloved ones, they reembarked on the S.S. *President Pierce.*

Rather typically, while my lot had fallen to serve in the occupied eastern region, Stanton's work had carried him to the Free West along with Cheloo University, which moved from Shantung to Szechwan. Stanton always lived on the frontier—be it in social and theological concepts or in circumstantial situation. In his wide range of influence among Chinese students, he preached a gospel of spiritual regeneration and Christian socialism. It was not surprising, then, that he should attach some hope to Chinese Communism and be one of the few missionaries to visit their headquarters in the caves of Yenan (North Shensi).

Out of his adventurous two months' journey and five days' contact with Communist leaders he appeared to have gained some real justification for his hopes. Apparently the cordial reception, all that he saw and heard, gave evidence to their declared aims of common freedom, justice, and democracy for the people. Besides, they seemed ready to give welcome to both the Y.M.C.A. and the Christian church.

To me, who from my narrow confines had tended to idealize the Free West, his direct report regarding both Communists and Nationalists raised the question whether some of us might not have been misjudging the intentions of the former and overvaluating the performance of the latter. No doubt, the responsible National Government,

under overwhelming economic strains, must have seemed
to be failing the people while also exercising excessively
bureaucratic powers.

As the months passed, our mode of living and our work
held a rather even keel. I could feel myself challenged and
bountifully occupied with departmental administration,
instruction, and student activities from day to day. A typical Sunday offered an array of opportunities: Eight A.M.
downtown student Bible class was followed by University
Church Chinese-language service; at eleven there was worship at the American Community Church (near our home)
with an early afternoon student social gathering in the
Fellowship Hall; after that it might become a choice between the Municipal Orchestra concert at the Lyceum
Theatre or a stroll among the flower beds of the alluring
French Park.

Among the pursuits of mind and spirit, there stands out
sharply a gem of a poem. Alice Duer Miller's *The White
Cliffs* (of Dover), 1941, by its sentiments of patriotism and
pathos unfolded in charming simplicity and sank deeply
into my heart. At a time when London so nobly battled for
its life, this sensitive portrayal of English character by an
American woman living in London, married to an English-
man, simply carried me away with the manner in which
she bound together the English-speaking peoples.

> The tree of Liberty grew and changed and spread,
>   But the seed was English.
>
>   I am American bred,
> I have seen much to hate here—much to forgive,
>   But in a world where England is finished and dead,
> I do not wish to live.

Similarly, in the realm of spiritual aspiration, I was at this time led to discover my favorite hymn. I found, for leading devotions at our annual Mission retreat, a ringing keynote for time and circumstance: "We Would Be Building" (Purd E. Deitz, 1935). What word or melody could speak more clearly our deepest yearnings?

> We would be building; temples still undone
>   O'er crumbling walls their crosses scarcely lift;
> Waiting till love can raise the broken stone,
>   And hearts creative bridge the human rift;
> We would be building, Master, let Thy plan
> Reveal the life that God would give to man.

This mood of spiritual resolve and expectation, matched to the appealing strains of Sibelius' "Finlandia," both melted and lifted our hearts.

An element in our domestic life, adding variety and flavor, was the occasional out-of-town guest. Most outstanding was the companionship of Harry Coldwell, Methodist missionary from Fukien, who lingered with us for three months while undergoing treatment for cataract. This energetic and versatile man had been marvelously combining early interests as a naturalist with his work of country evangelism. He found those long itineraries, mostly through the mountains on foot, could never become wearisome or dull. The American Museum of Natural History has thereby been enriched with his collection of 22,000 specimens of Fukien birds and butterflies, accompanied by authoritative works. Also excelling as a hunter, strictly humanitarian, he carried us along with his exciting experiences, already recorded in his book, *The Blue Tiger* (of Fukien). This stealthy creature, terrorizing the villages,

snatching away goats, dogs, and sometimes children, had
finally been hunted down. His tiger-shooting record stood
at thirty-four.

By mid-1941 we felt the sharp winds of change. Increasing delay and uncertainty of mails, due to reduced shipping, was touching a tender spot. Instead of a fortnight,
delivery required from four to six weeks. Then some relief
was afforded by the "Clipper" airmail delivery to Manila,
which, however, still depended on connecting ships to
Shanghai. Later a more ingenious and direct method
turned up for bridging the woeful gap in family communication. It became known as the "missionary mailbag."
Norman Page of the San Francisco KGEI radio station introduced the plan, as we learned, and managed the send-
ing of personal messages for direct reception in Shanghai.
Any of the separated family members, having returned to
the United States, might provide brief greetings or any urgent information, which was then broadcast from Treasure
Island during the hours of five to seven Sunday mornings.
But ten to twelve P.M. was our time to cling to the radio
set in hopes of hearing our names called. Even though not
fortunate enough to be included, one was still thrilled to
share messages coming across to local friends. I fared less
favorably than my partners, hearing only once from Grace
—the family having resided in Canada part of the time.
The cheering news was that they had become settled in
Ann Arbor, Michigan.

10

WHILE SHANGHAI WAITS

$\mathcal{T}$HE FACTOR in the emerging situation of 1941 that concerned us more and more was the ominous mounting of international tension. Japan kept boldly challenging the vital principles and interests of the West. Now, Shanghai, always exposing a sensitive nerve to sharp East-West confrontations, began to show the jitters. Were we moving on a course of impending collision? Several factors seemed so to indicate: Embattled China strongly urged action by the ABC bloc—the American, British, and Chinese anti-aggression coalition; Japan was swiftly consolidating her advance position in Indochina and began at this time to operate under a reorganized cabinet of predominant military control; meanwhile, on the European axis front (Tokyo had joined the Berlin-Rome axis in 1940), the colossal German war machine was battling desperately against the terrific Russian drive.

Late 1941 pressed the hour of decision for American and British policy in Asia. The unabating military expansion of Japan in the southeast Pacific regions was fast presenting an intolerable threat. Charges and recriminations flew back and forth. In Washington, President Roosevelt insisted on the principles of territorial integrity and com-

mercial equality, and Ambassador Grew spoke out sharply
in Tokyo—"straight from the horse's mouth," with the decisive result of freezing Japanese assets in the United
States and terminating trade. On the other hand, Tokyo's
accusations blamed America for obstructing the creation
of the East Asia Co-prosperity Sphere. Furthermore, Japanese military spokesmen warned threateningly of retaliation against American communities in the Far East if the
New Order in China was not accepted.

Personally, I began to see a real confrontation as an in-
evitability. Hostilities might be very near. Nevertheless, it
still seemed, as long as the Germans had no decisive victory over Russia and while in Tokyo the liberals (including the Emperor) retained some influence in the cabinet,
Japan would not rashly precipitate a general Pacific war.
Could there still be a way to stem the tide?

I was discovering, during these crisis years, that my op-
timistic philosophy of peace and war was undergoing considerable revision. I faced the harsh realities of raw human
nature and the pressures of national self-interest. The
question: Can our noble institutions of democratic government and presumed sentiments of international goodwill, supported by a body of international law and imple-
mented by a League of Nations, stand before the upsurg-
ing forces of extreme nationalism and rampant militancy?
I began to see in our one world great evils on the march
that must be opposed and sacred rights trampled upon
which must be fought for. Would it bring a dark age or
one of heroic struggle?

Within the memory of recent years loomed vivid experiences, giving shape to my thought. In the summer of
1936 I had joined the Sherwood Eddy International Relations Seminar, touring major countries of Europe. In Ge-
neva, in the League of Nations Assembly Hall I sat down

with much feeling in the seat reserved for Haile Selassie, ruler of Ethiopia, whose country was being ravished by Italian Fascist armies, as the League stood helpless to prevent or to punish aggression. In Berlin, in a well-secluded hotel room, a group of us were listening with bated breath to a finding of Reinhold Niebuhr. For weeks he had been examining closely the prospects of the German Nazi situation. "Fellows," he began in a hushed voice, "I'm distressed to tell you, we shall have to fight the war with Germany all over again." As to Russia, I had ranged from Shanghai across Siberia and traveled both north and south from Moscow observing the new social experiments of the Soviet Union. Much seemed apparent that showed the vision and will and creativeness to construct a society of a new pattern for the world to see and perhaps to emulate (to be sure, mine was a partial view). German Nazism, in contrast, boasted a racial superiority and had a mind of belligerency that struck at the heart of civilization. Then, in August, 1940, my heart burdened with the horrors of Japan's aggression in China and the degenerating effects of militarism upon her own society, I gazed from the steamship deck upon the booming port of Nagasaki, and into my mind came the sober thought: There is a cosmic justice operating in the world. Surely, Japan cannot continue in her mistaken course. The time for aping the century-old imperialisms is past. Unless she can shortly curb these ignoble ambitions and amend her ways—I can see this strategic city blasted to bits!

So now, in the midst of Shanghai's rising fever, I had begun to feel committed to the probability of an East-West showdown, and consequently implied this in letters to the family. Apparently, Grace, on yon side of the ocean, had been experiencing similar forebodings; for in a letter posted many weeks before, in her indirect but reassuring way she wrote: "If emergency would arise here, we are prepared to take it."

Nevertheless, at this time I sensed a critical situation arising within the family, pertaining particularly to Grace's health. Although communication, so intermittent and long-awaited, gave only veiled suggestion, my concern deepened as I realized that her physical energy and emotional stability were being undermined. It seemed apparent that my family was needing me. Yet, in consideration of her rigid code of duty and remarkable fortitude, it was doubtful that she would expect me to leave my post. Finally, in response to my appeal for a decision on what seemed best, I got the word (this time within three weeks): "Yes, come if you can and if the ocean is safe enough." After the Mission's full consideration to my urgent request, an agreement was reached that home leave might be arranged for January, 1942. Ocean passage by neutral shipping, though limited, was still considered feasible. But apparently Grace's concern arose from experiencing the hazardous voyage on the Canadian liner *Empress of Asia,* December, 1940. Pursued by German submarines, the Canadian vessel had precariously zigzagged her uncertain course across the high seas. For me, barring a sharp turn of events, no such risks would be involved; so I proceeded to adjust my work and pack my trunk for a projected six-month furlough, hopeful of bringing relief to the family—and possibly returning to Shanghai.

December 8, 1941, we awoke to the echoes that shook the world. Aroused at dawn by artillery boom, we gasped at the horrific news of Pearl Harbor, and the word that the Settlement was now being occupied. In the midst of active diplomatic negotiations, Japan's dastardly sneak attack had struck like a bolt of lightning upon the sleeping American naval base at Hawaii. The die was cast! The official radio message from the American Consulate ran something like this: "Japan, without warning, has attacked Pearl Harbor, causing vast destruction and has issued a declaration of war against the United States and Great Britain. The International Settlement is now in the process of being taken over without any resistance excepting the few early shots by a British gunboat. All nationals are requested to remain calmly at their homes until the situation can be clarified."

Suddenly, for me, the family problem had dissolved. I was clearly in no position to do anything about it, but could only commit everything into the Heavenly Father's hands. On February 21 an airmail letter from Grace came through (dated November 18). It brought a slightly more encouraging report, at least not alarming, which contributed greatly toward peace of mind. I immediately sent reply, assuring her we were still busy and buoyant, rejoicing in service. "God bless you and keep each of you in his everlasting care." To this I felt the necessity of adding, "This may be the last letter for a very long time."

Remarkably enough, Shanghai did not panic. Accepting the inevitable, with a minimum of confusion, almost directly business resumed and administration carried on. The second day, favored by fog and drizzle, I ventured out; after taking a tram downtown, under cover of umbrella and raincoat I continued mingling among the Chinese on the streets. Traversing the central area of Nanking Road and the Bund, I perceived no evidence of Japanese military control, until on North Szechwan Road I witnessed the take-over of our popular downtown haunt, the United States Navy Y.M.C.A. Within me I said sadly, Good-by Navy Y.

As to our university, we regathered the classes after a week's suspension and hastily brought our term's work to conclusion, not a little surprised that such was even possible. The joint educational enterprise folded up, leaving faculty and students to disperse as they could, most of them finding ways of trekking off southwesterly into the "free" area. My Chinese associate in political science, Dr. Tung, by putting on the appearance of a traveling merchant, managed to cross through the enemy lines without suspicion. Actually, he was on his way to join the Supreme National Defense Council in Chungking. President Lee, back from a year's study in America, decided on another venture. This time he chose the mountain area of western Fukien Province, where the secluded town of Shao-wu became the reassembling place for a remnant of Hangchow staff and students. His wife and two daughters remaining in Shanghai, he had taken with him the only son, still in his teens, thus balancing the separated family. This precious boy shortly thereafter fell victim to the dreaded cholera, laying a burden of grief and loneliness upon the devoted father. For me, along with others of the missionary staff, the doors were open for private tutoring in our homes, especially for assisting senior students to complete their courses and for supervising their graduation theses, so that degrees could be granted.

Transocean communication had really struck a dead end. So it appeared, at least, if one did not take account of the human factor in Chinese administrative practice. Our profound gratitude went to those loyal postal clerks, ingeniously finding avenues for getting letters off, now and then, via Manila or Chungking. A more certain if not more direct way opened late in June when Shanghai hosted the thrilling event—repatriation of Americans. With these departing friends, all being brought into port from various interior places, we rejoiced at their deliverance and happy home-going. No one residing in Shanghai was to be included, except a few special cases of critical state of health. The Van Everas from Hangchow undertook to convey my verbal greetings and deliver my letter to the anxious family. On the Italian S.S. *Conte Verde,* under International Red Cross supervision, off they sailed for Lorenzo Marque on the East African coast, from there to be transferred to the Swedish liner M.S. *Gripsholm,* destined for New York. Presently, among us Shanghailanders, a rumor began to spread and a hope: a second repatriation! Could we pin our faith on the returning *Conte Verde?*

A British repatriation occurred in August, whereby outgoing American mail was accepted. Thereafter came also a few chances to send a twenty-word message on a special Red Cross letter form. Incoming mail became extremely rare. We practically ceased to expect any and were simply overjoyed to be handed a letter. Early in May I had received one from Grace, and after a gap of nearly six months another came in late August after having lingered four months on the way.

What was by now transpiring in the fabric and soul of Shanghai? No longer an international island of refuge and an open door to the outside world, but waiting for the unknown and hoping for the better, the refuge city of the Orient had entered into the fateful hour of life and death. Everywhere were evident symptoms of her overbearing illness and her progressive deterioration. By the loss of her precious freedom, Shanghai was turning into an isolated, terrified, impoverished, and ravished body politic. People kept fleeing by the thousands. The serious shortage of rice and mounting food costs, attended by inflation, black-marketing and merciless profiteering, laid appalling distress upon the masses and grave responsibility upon the Settlement Municipal Council.

Obviously, the Japanese take-over introduced into our

social order considerable political and administrative changes, and as for ourselves, placed us in the position of enemy residents. British and American representatives on the Municipal Council were speedily replaced with Germans and Italians, while related diplomatic and Red Cross matters became the function of the Swiss Consulate. Utilities, banks, and business concerns acquired new masters—though in many cases the new bosses operated behind the scenes.

Very soon we were caught in the economic pinch. With personal bank accounts and all Mission funds being frozen, I had to resort to the sale of unused household items such as the sewing machine and refrigerator, as a means of carrying on. But it seemed apparent that some common arrangement would be necessary for sustaining the American residents, of which over a thousand remained. Already several hundred were gathering for food and shelter on the Shanghai American School compound, which became the SAS Relief Station—with Fatty Hansen, retired chef of the Navy Y, in full charge of the kitchen.

October 1 dated the official "enemy alien" registration. Hereafter, each was adorned with a brilliant red armband, labeling us as belonging to the enemy and specifying nationality and number. Strict regulations required that these be worn unfailingly anywhere outside of the home, making us publicly conspicuous and somewhat restricted in movement. We were truly "marked men." But, turning to the other side of the coin, we found ample occasions to feel rewarded—a consequence that the Japanese could hardly have suspected. It was the gleam of favor and friendship in the eyes of many passing Chinese. As an intimate friend put it, "Now everybody can see that you are joined with us in the ABC Club" (American, British, Chinese). We carried the badge of honorable status! At the same time we realized the necessity of caution in our associations, particularly so because of the host of spying Nazi advisers and their henchmen. No more student Bible classes picnicked on our secluded lawn, nor did the choir group gather around our piano. To have the privilege of the public library and access to the parks seemed adequate, along with Sunday worship service and the daily attending to household business. Reading in this spare time included such books as: Shirer's *Berlin Diary*, Niebuhr's *Christianity and Power Politics*, H. G. Wells's *Autobiography*, Steinbeck's *Grapes of Wrath*, Hemingway's *For Whom the Bell Tolls*, and Cronin's *Keys of the Kingdom*.

In our household (Dr. Whitlock had joined us), as the weeks passed, we managed somehow to keep up standards of health. American cereals, cornmeal, and cracked wheat were available by ration at the Red Cross station, and likewise a small daily portion of white bread at the bakery, while for spread we depended mainly on cocoa butter. Fresh vegetables and meats were very uncertain, since farmers refused to bring in supplies to the Japanese-controlled markets. Was there any breakfast coffee? Oh, yes, there was still in stock a special variety, labeled "Bean Perfect Mixture."

The *Conte Verde* had already brought back its load of returning Japanese and resumed its stand at the Bund—surely this meant repatriation. My little wardrobe trunk had stood packed for months, and some select household articles had been placed in the care of special Chinese friends with fixed residence in the city. (Most recent orders now forbade removal of any effects.) To this extent I was in readiness to leave on short notice. Or, had our Christian witness of standing by not yet been fulfilled?

There was another harassing factor that everyone faced. We became increasingly aware that the ills befallen Shang-

hai were cutting much deeper than economics or bare sub-
sistence. The most heinous thing threatening the life of
both Settlement and Concession was the injection of violent political gangsterism. The Wang Ching-wei puppet
regime in Nanking began thrusting in its sinister hand to
destroy personal freedom and security. It took the form of
strong-arm measures to compel support by wealthy and influential Chinese, the most direct blow falling upon the
press. Woe to journalists who dared to voice opposition to
Japanese policies! One heard of men disappearing myste-
riously, then rumors of horrible inquisition at No. 76 Jess-
field Road, and later resort to open assassination. Our first
terrible shock came with the death of Herman Liu. This
personal friend and honored Christian scholar, president
of the University of Shanghai, for no discoverable reason
had suffered a fatal shot as he stepped from a public bus.
Soon after, the editor of the *Evening Post*, Mr. Chang, was
gunned from behind while having afternoon tea in a German restaurant, and more gruesome was the fate of Mr.
Wong, assistant editor of the Chinese daily *Shun Pao*,
whose decapitated body had been discovered at a dark
street corner.

British and American press personnel, equally hated and
sometimes threatened, were known to have been black-
listed for early deportation. The outstanding case that
deeply impressed us was that of J. B. Powell, the coura-
geous American editor of the noted *Shanghai Weekly Review*. Considerable mystery had attended Powell's disap-
pearance just weeks after Japanese occupation and then
there were rumors of his being included in the June repatriation due to critical state of health. In whispers, people
spoke of his incarceration in the notorious Bridge House
and later in the Kiangwan Prison Hospital—but details no
one seemed to know. What we had at this point come to

know was the stark fact that no one could feel exempt from the nefarious activities of the Japanese Secret Police. People were being whisked away, and a hushed phrase became current: "Yes, the Bridge House!" With prayerful concern for our fellow missionary, Will Hudspeth, of the British Bible Society, who had recently fallen victim, we anxiously pondered, Now, who next?

The evening of November 3 passed by with the ordinary routine. A few lively rounds of Crokinole suited the mood after supper, before each entered for a while his own private world in a book of fiction. Then, prior to retiring came the huddle for review and appraisal of the day's happenings, attended with a bit of crystal gazing into the unknown. Committed to the steadfast assurance of providential care (Ps. 121:8), as usual, we filed up the staircase performing our little ritual. Each, with upraised hand, passed along the word "Excelsior."

11

POLITICAL PRISONER

𝒯HE HOUR was five thirty next morning. I found myself awakened by a bit of a stir and a mumble of voices down in the hall. Then came a soft rap on my bedroom door and the grave face of our servant appeared. He announced simply, "The Japanese have come for you." Somewhat in a daze, I swung out of bed to face realities—which were just a few steps away. So began for me an entirely new drama within the context and contingencies of missions and war.

The arresting Japanese officer, attended by a French policeman (French Concession) and a Chinese in civilian clothes, handed me a slip of paper. On the top I saw clearly spelled out my name and number, with underneath it the official notification: "You are to be interned immediately at No. 372 Haiphong Road." Well, that was it; but I had no inkling what to expect at Haiphong Road. Yet I realized a mildness, even courtesy, in their manner that allayed apprehension. Especially when told that I might take a small suitcase of clothing, toilet articles, books (naming Bible), blanket, and a little money, I felt assured of not being headed for the Bridge House.

A further surprise came when, after dressing, shaving, and packing, I was advised to take breakfast (the servant had eggs and toast already prepared) and carry along a couple of sandwiches. In the meantime, none of my fellow residents made appearance, prudently avoiding any complications. Apparently, they were not among the chosen. Finally, Whit (Dr. Whitlock), who had recently joined us, peeked from his slightly opened door and in that manner secretly saw me off!

As we walked out of the compound gate, the Chinese attendant, in the act of offering to carry my blanket, took occasion to whisper, "Why did you not get out of Shanghai while there was a chance?" Not expecting a reply, he was simply sharing a fellow feeling, which I deeply appreciated. Yet, his words implied also a question that puzzled him and to me expressed a sort of rebuke. Here was shown that concern for the safety of the mission worker coupled with bewilderment at his folly which had become a common reaction among the suffering Chinese of Hangchow.

Having been conducted to the local gendarmerie station, I became one in a gloom-laden group of about fifty men similarly picked up and equally perplexed. Shortly, they packed us into open military trucks and, by groups, hauled us off.

The mysterious No. 372 Haiphong Road turned out to be the vacated American marine barracks. Now it became our prison camp. This layout, containing a two-story brick building, a small one alongside, and a fairly serviceable mess hall, was securely enclosed by board fence and barbed wire. Once within the bayonet-guarded gate, one felt little sense of connection with the outside world. By noon, the widely cast gendarmerie net had gathered in 350 so-called dangerous characters, all presumably under suspicion of offense against Imperial Japan.

After being shuffled around for hours, repeatedly checked for names, numbered off, and grouped, we were called to assembly before Colonel Odera, commandant in charge. Avoiding military brusqueness, this man of past middle age began by urging patience and calmness. Then, pointedly, he announced basic principles and conditions: First, that we were brought here for reason of military necessity and for our own personal safety; second, that our essential daily needs would be provided for as long as we obeyed regulations of the camp; third, that any attempt to escape would be dealt with most severely.

Sizing up our commandant, I began to feel somewhat assured of decency and moderation in camp control, with due regard for humanity and code of international law. Now we knew our status to be definitely that of prisoners of war. So, in view of being incarcerated on political grounds, our being held under control of the army might well be delivering us from a worse fate. Official records were made out within several days, including forms for personal history, along with photographs and fingerprints on criminal record sheets. Besides, each signed a statement promising not to attempt escape.

The inmates of our camp, which after a couple of weeks increased to 360, proved to be predominately of British nationality. Americans rated one fifth, Netherlanders a score, and Greeks a dozen. Ages ranging from twenty-one to seventy-four (some in feeble health) added to the perplexity regarding basis of choice. Really, no consistent explanation for the personal selections could be found, not even that our group was designed as a roundup of influential enemy aliens. Truly, our compact community represented a rather rich variety of professions and pursuits: municipal officials, police inspectors, customs and postal commissioners, business executives, bankers, lawyers, journalists, engineers, teachers, clergymen, and physicians (ten of us being missionaries). Among other numerous nondescripts not included in this roster of Shanghai's Bad Boys, it would be foolhardy not to suspect a Quisling or two.

Within basic military provisions, the camp readily became organized for self-regulation and maintenance. Major responsibility was assumed by our pair of Shanghai industrialists: Mr. Collar (British) of Imperial Chemicals and Mr. Henningson (American) of Shanghai Bakery and Confectionery. Only through these two men could the captains of our thirty-one rooms, singly or collectively, bring to the Japanese authorities matters of concern. Similarly, through these channels came our instructions. The system worked well, and great credit was due our worthy leaders and room captains, who took the brunt.

Room 30, eyed by all as a choice location, by some magic fell to the group to which I had been assigned. This second-floor level, southern exposure with glass-paneled doors opening on a narrow railed-in veranda, offered cheerful sunshine and a view of the grounds and gate. Twenty camp cots, closely set and allowing a narrow aisle down the middle, made a very congested den, greatly relieved, however, by the traditional spirit of British good sportsmanship. All had been total strangers to me, including the two Canadians. But what clinched the fine fellowship happened a week after. Our captain gave word, "Squeeze in one more cot." Then, who should I see walk in but Steve Sturton from Hangchow! He and Bishop Curtis (Anglican) had been arrested and brought out to join our company of Shanghai Bad Boys.

In terms of military classification, presumably, our camp rated with that of officers, requiring no outside labor. Prison duties were thus confined to maintaining the establishment in good order and meeting our personal needs from such resources as were made available. Hardly any of us found fatigue duty burdensome. This provided a

rather agreeable means for regular physical activity and
gave each a share in the cooperative system, which was
becoming our way of life.

Aside from the matter of matching professional abilities
to particular needs, there remained quite a range of choice.
Pat Gibbons (next bunk), Shanghai Power Company engineer, took over the heating system—if and when a little
coal could be had. Webber, the old-time sailor, could
scarcely meet the demand for mending cot canvasses. The
accommodating banker, Mr. Gordon, volunteered outright
for the "lowdown": "Unless somebody beats me to it, I'll
take charge of the latrine." He got his wish! I decided to
join the group for the mess hall, not for the cooking but
for the cleanup. Bishop Curtis and I stuck to the scullery
squad, daily scrubbing pots and pans with sand for lack of
soap. To our company of several squads fell the honorable
name of Panhandlers. In consequence, when graduating
from this Haiphong Camp (Institute), after serving three
hundred days internship, I proudly accepted the awarded
Ph.D.

Our day began at six thirty A.M. and ended with lights
out at nine thirty P.M. Properly dressed and with room in
good order, we paraded at seven for morning inspection
and roll call. This outdoor pre-breakfast performance was
repeated in the evening at seven in our room, always being introduced by a brief report from the captain, followed
by a rapid numbering off—all in Japanese. Since respectful
bowing rated so high in Nipponese custom and military
regulations, our slovenly ways occasionally brought forth
a special disciplinary drill.

Having to depend upon Japanese military rations alone
would have proved hazardous to health, especially in view
of their low quality. The most nourishing item, indeed our
greatest boon, was the bowl of American cracked wheat

for breakfast. This was known to be coming from the great store of Red Cross cereals in Shanghai, all of it confiscated by the Japanese army, depriving thousands of Chinese starving refugees in that society from which we were now set apart. At the same time, we had reason to suspect the quartermaster of filching a portion of our assigned ration for supplementing that of the company of thirty soldiers at the guardhouse.

From the very beginning we had realized the helping hand of the Red Cross. During the first few days of disorganization and the process of getting mess-hall equipment put into usable shape, food was permitted to be brought in to us by the British and American Associations. Enormous tin cans of nourishing stew, hailed by cheers on arrival, carried us along on two feeds a day. A bowl apiece became a feast. The Red Cross also supplied the entire camp with used folding cots, and shortly thereafter each of us was favored with a newly made sleeping pad.

Fortunately, also, we were not to be deprived of medical care, since we had among our number two highly qualified physicians. Dr. T. B. Dunn, known for long practice among the American community in Shanghai, immediately opened a clinic and was soon joined by Dr. Sturton from Hangchow. Our gratitude to these men had no bounds. In cooperation with the Japanese medical officer (who also attended the regular military camp), limited Red Cross supplies were obtained, testing facilities set up, and a hospital room arranged in camp. As a general precaution, each man was given a weekly check on his weight, resulting in a serious t.b. case's being transferred within the first month to the Shanghai Police Hospital. Eye and dental care, which appeared very unlikely, later also became available and in my case served to provide replacement for a broken front tooth. In close relation to these health care services, many of us participated in a professionally directed (by one of our group) physical training class that afforded scientific discipline in deep breathing, muscle control, and eye exercise. I found it bracing and relaxing.

Then, there was the problem of leisure time. Idleness in our circumscribed world would surely breed a morbid state of mind or a flare of rebellion. We realized this, as likewise did Colonel Odera, who called an assembly to address us on the point. The good advice he tendered, in obvious sincerity and with real concern, came to us in free English translation: "Men, do not consume yourselves, but begin to construct something." Indeed, I could see no point to an attitude of futility and gloom; rather, I clearly set my objectives on maintaining health, keeping the mind stimulated, performing cooperative service, and retaining a hopeful outlook. This might, perhaps, be considered as corresponding to the Biblical account of putting down four anchors and wishing for the day (Acts 27:29).

In the first place, personal needs, though simple, absorbed considerable time due to inconvenience. Were it mere face-wash and shave or turn at the showers, one always crept up in a line. Our regular laundering chores became an exercise of skill as well as patience—processing underwear, towel, and sheet in one of those half-dozen little round washbowls. I reckoned the urgency of the timely stitch for clothing upkeep. For example, my two precious suits of long woolen underwear, serving day and night throughout the winter, had by spring each acquired a dozen patches. It also became a sort of communal sport to mend shirts or trousers with a crazy-patch design of colors and angles.

Opportunities for recreation were not entirely lacking. On the occasional sunny afternoon, permission was given to use the adjoining enclosed lot for a lusty match in football and lively cheering on the sidelines. We could also assemble for early evening song-fests or even the rare dramatic entertainment. For many of us, the two prized gifts sent in from the outside were an old piano and several shelves of used books. The way thus opened for study classes and concert talent. High on my list of worthwhile volumes stood Galsworthy's depictions of the Victorian era by his lucid fiction in trilogy form—*The Forsyte Saga, The Patrician, The Silver Spoon*. And if there arose any fear that our pool of knowledge might become exhausted, we could gather assurance from that solid old set of *Encyclopaedia Britannica*.

Beginning with January, 1943, a small relief fund became available. Through the Swiss Consulate, each one who so desired could receive from his respective government a monthly loan equivalent to eight dollars in U.S. currency. Through the pooling of a portion of these funds the food committee could from time to time provide potatoes or other extra vegetables, with now and then a bit of ham or an egg. Also we managed to open a canteen, providing a few essentials: toilet articles, extra cigarettes (a pack a week on ration), simple items of clothing, such as socks, and the special luxury of a small allotment of peanut butter and jam for adding a little embellishment to the coarse brown bread.

About this time, also, through the mediation of tactful camp leaders, permission was granted for us to list urgently needed clothing and bedding and to provide an address from which such might be obtained. While we still lacked any direct communication, what a blessing it was to begin receiving these treasures (comforter, sheets, pillow, overcoat, rubber overshoes, and a few other items) and have the feeling of not being totally cut off!

To the conducting of Sunday morning worship service we met no hindrance. In fact, the presence among us of two bishops and a high-ranking Salvation Army man might be interpreted as anticipating this spiritual exercise. These leading clergymen were: Bishop John Curtis (Anglican), Bishop Ralph Ward (American Methodist), Brigadier Walker (British Salvation Army), and also Will H. Hudspeth (British and Foreign Bible Society). Truly, these modest assemblings for giving witness to our faith, heeding the Holy Word, and giving glory to the Eternal God brought spiritual light and strength to many of us.

Picture a Sunday morning scene at daybreak, as it was customary for Bishop Curtis to administer the Holy Sacrament of bread and wine. Perhaps ten or twelve of us are seated on a pair of crude benches in the general hall. Outside, the bugle call is followed by the sharp click-clack of measured strides, indicating the hour for changing of the guard. Now the venerable bishop is slipping on his priestly vestment, having already arranged in front of us a small table with white cloth and sacramental elements. Together we are entering into the spirit of the Eucharist, transcending time and circumstance. Is it prison camp or upper room? We follow the leading voice, "Now hear what comfortable words our Savior Christ saith: 'Come unto me all ye that travail and are heavy laden, and I will refresh you.'" Four at a time we kneel upon the folded gray blanket on the floor, gratefully partaking of the mystic elements. "This do, as often as you drink it, in remembrance of me. . . . The peace of God which passeth understanding, keep your hearts and minds."

Thus led into a sense of union with the Eternal Goodness, one could likewise feel a special closeness with loved ones, although oceans apart. How could any of us doubt the ultimate victory of right or even bear in our hearts any thought of hatred against those called our enemies?

Nevertheless, by stark realities, we were strictly prisoners. Each one of us was selectively incarcerated, kept in severe isolation from outside contact, held under the strain of mystery and apprehension as to the nature of the charge against us—and not at all secure from the clutches of the devilish Secret Police. Under such range of distressing factors attending our camp life, no largeness of spirit and art of accommodation could successfully banish our daily anxieties.

For myself, I was unable to grasp what purpose was being served by our rather severe isolation. Was it punishment or precaution or just the ways of war? Of things transpiring in the city and of the world situation, especially war developments, we had the scantest knowledge, having access only to a small local Japanese newspaper. Even at that, the almost daily reports of Imperial victories on land or sea could become revealing to one who knew his geography. Frequently they disclosed advances in the reverse! As to allowing any visits to the prison camp, this appeared out of the question. However, by the end of three months the gate was set slightly ajar, permitting each of us to have a visitor—family member or close friend. An exciting moment it was when I glimpsed Ed (Dr. Walline) being ushered through the gateway and then received the summons to meet him in the guardhouse. We had ten wonderful minutes together. Disregarding the eyes and ears of a close-standing officer, we restored the broken link with a homey chat and banished my ghost of isolation. A few months later Miss Margaret Frame (also of the China Council) managed to favor me with a brief visit, a privilege that only a few of us enjoyed. These contacts proved decidedly bracing and also established the hope that hereby some encouraging word might somehow reach my family. Still later, after seven months in camp, we were finally permitted to send out one twenty-five-word International Red Cross letter for overseas delivery—the first opportunity for communication with my beloved kindred. Eagerly, I sent a message to Grace in Ann Arbor, indicating my situation and giving assurance of continued well-being. From Stanton and parents (Kitchener, Ontario), I received a Red Cross form letter. From Grace, however, nothing was ever delivered.

One of the puzzling factors, always overhanging and still unclarified, pertained to the nature of my crime. Specific grounds for my incarceration remained a mystery. As everyone else, I had earlier been summoned for interrogation; this, in my case, proved brief and superficial, supplying no inkling as to the charges. Many of our inmates had some previous connections with the armed services of their country or other military-political involvements. Dr. Sturton, for example, served as surgeon in the British Navy (World War I) and as previously mentioned performed medical service (International Red Cross) in the Chinese Nationalist Army (1928), which brought him into close relationship with Chiang Kai-shek. For myself, I could not think of any suspicious connections that might cause offense. Yet, one could never know. Japanese war psychology had reached such a nervous passion for ferreting and clamping dangerous thoughts that, by report, as many as fifty thousand of their own people had been subjected to arrest and detention as political offenders. Again, at the moment of arrest, some of our men were told that this was an act of retaliation for mistreatment accorded Japanese residing in Allied countries.

The truly evil thing that ceaselessly plagued our prison camp, holding everyone in jeopardy, was the sinister interference of the Secret Police. This suddenly whisking a man or two away to suffer the ordeal of inquisition kept all nerves in strain. Actually, not more than 10 percent of our number were thus taken out. Bishop Ralph Ward was one of them. Always they came back—some in a day or two, others in weeks—in various states of nervous and physical breakdown and totally silent as to what had gone on. A most appalling situation struck us in August. It was the case of a robust British police inspector, who after ten days of obvious torture was brought back to camp and carried into the clinic in a condition much more dead than alive. Within two days he died. This was too dreadful! Camp indignation flared up to riot pitch. Colonel Odera, far from condoning such treatment at the hands of the gendarmerie, and being responsible for camp discipline, had real occasion to take alarm. Appeasingly, he undertook to offer more assurance of protection and at the same time issued stern warning against any disorder.

12

HO FOR REPATRIATION

*B*Y THIS TIME we were aware of significant outside developments. In April, 1943, all enemy aliens had been interned in what were officially called Civil Assembly Centers, our missionary group being gathered at the Chapei Camp. Unlike Haiphong, which was directly under the army, these camps were set up and administered under consular jurisdiction and based on the principle of families' bringing with them necessary personal and household effects and making arrangements for food supplies. Communications were restricted to a fifty-word intercamp letter once a month (including our camp). To us, such a privilege of local correspondence spelled a real gain; another bar was lowered! Out of the big move came to me a real surprise, when two of my suitcases, well packed, arrived in camp for me to claim. What could it mean? Perhaps it flashed the dawn glimmer of repatriation!

Always there had stood the question, How long? With little chance that our camp, though of special character, might be disbanded, what hope there was lay in repatriation—otherwise, it would be "for the duration." However, this preoccupation sprouted a crop of fanciful ideas, none of which included attempt to escape. The prize guess was credited to Winkelmann (son of the commander-in-chief of the Dutch army). Sportive as usual, he offered a scientific answer: "Now just figure it out for yourself. In the first three months we've had three men die—in thirty years we'll all be out of here."

Promisingly, by early September rumors for that second repatriation were thriving in earnest, though for Americans only. One of the problems related to the *Conte Verde*. This vessel of our hope had by now been scuttled in the Shanghai harbor, the crew aiming to prevent Japanese take-over when Italy dropped out of the war. As arrangements proceeded, tentative lists showed names from our group (much secrecy!). It meant a trying time and the passing around of hushed reports, reminding us of "One is taken and the other left." Finally, confirmed listing named forty-two men, and the ailing Bishop Ward, most regrettably, was not included.

September 19, 1943, the day of departure arrived. Passing through the gateway, after 319 days of imprisonment, still could hardly bring an experience of elation, but rather a mood of gratitude and reflection. Our pathway of deliverance was solidly bordered with noble men, not accorded the favor that we were, yet cheering us a hearty send-off. Forty-two of us were being released and restored to the normal life of the larger world; while there remained 318 in their wretched confinement, destined to endure for time unknown that restricted, lonely, and precarious life!

In my heart there burned a parting appeal from a very dear British friend who had encountered the worst: "For God's sake, do what you can to get our governments to deal with these diabolical police agents." I had also learned anew how, within the magnitude of God's providence, distressful situations often bear hidden meanings. Here the treasury of my faith became again enriched. The choicest example emerged from the experience of Will Hudspeth, who had been thrust into the notorious Bridge House political prison back in October, 1942, and for whom we then had such grave and prayerful concern. Mercifully, he had been released to Haiphong Road Camp and become one of us. Without disclosing the horrible hardships suffered during the long weeks of incarceration, he did relate to me a dramatic incident bespeaking the marvels of the Spirit. Apparently in a state of utter wretchedness and near loss of hope, he caught one day a glint of sympathy in the eye of his seemingly impassive guard. Then followed an amazing revelation and a gentle rebuke, in words something like this: "Friend," whispered the guard, "you should not be so disheartened. You are a Christian. I am one also and have day by day been watching over you. Now, just take courage. Soon you will be released from here." So wonderfully and truly spoke this common khaki-clad man, as though it were a white-robed angel bringing the message. Ah, is there ever a place so evil that Christian love and hope cannot dwell therein?—often in unsuspected guise.

In gratitude, I passed on to Will Hudspeth my treasured little volume, *Living Every Day,* by Joseph Fort Newton, which along with my Bible I had brought with me into camp. (Only the Bible could be carried out.) I deeply cherished the fine fellowship of Room 30, especially remembering the complete sharing of the few and meager Christmas parcels. Also, I carried a gratifying sense of partaking (though removed) in the sufferings of the Chinese people.

So, now, with prison camp behind me and no criminal charges ever laid, I could only surmise as to what had brought me in. The most likely explanation would be mistaken identity. Several such cases were known, leading me to believe they were after my brother Stanton. The Japanese, being fiercely anti-Communist, undoubtedly had record of his tour to the Communist headquarters at Yenan and thus had him marked as a dangerous enemy and also a prospective source of useful information. Otherwise, I might fall back on the possibility of being selected by chance. Perhaps we three Canadians were needed for implementing the plan for prisoner exchange, making it possible to bring back highly skilled Japanese held in a Canadian detention camp. The question had become academic.

First, a thrilling bus ride to the Bund marked our leap from seclusion to public life and brought a renewed sense of identity with the common civil society. In confinement, only sun, moon and stars remained to me visible symbols of a world order that embraced us all. What meaning was there to the locomotive's call and the blast of the departing ship except a taunting reminder of our immobility? Next, while on the tender proceeding to the wharf, I glimpsed the half-sunken *Conte Verde,* and then viewed our exchange ship, the Japanese *Teia Maru,* bearing on her broadside the great red symbols of mercy. In the flush of my reinitiation into the normal society of household pals, scores of old friends, and especially the company of women and children, I plunged with zest into the service of carrying baggage on board. This continued far into the night. Finally there arrived the rather bedraggled company of over two hundred from the North China Weihsien Camp, having had three hard days on a rumbling train, and now full of excitement. Also, the while, I shared a situation of deep distress. Hille Arthur, critically ill, lay on a stretcher in the freight shed. His helplessness raised the question of being admitted on board. Finally, after full assurance by doctors and nurses among the passengers that they would be responsible for professional care, he was provided with a private cabin.

The *Teia Maru*, brilliantly lighted from bow to stern, steamed out of Shanghai September 20 at dawn with over 1200 passengers, some of whom had been taken on in Japan. At the same time, space was being reserved for adding 220 at stops farther on. This small freighter (formerly French) was reconstructed by the Japanese for troop transport but was not entirely seaworthy. Never had I imagined a crowded condition like that sweltering hold. Bunks three tiers high and barely shoulder wide offered little invitation for movement and scant space for breath. However, as men from the Haiphong Road Camp, it was our own choice to go down there. We called it the Glory Hole.

The voyage, though officially under International Red Cross supervision, afforded only such limited accommodations as the Japanese would or could provide. With understaffed crew they manned the ship and handled the food; beyond which, within general regulations, a system of self-management prevailed in matters of activities and safety. (There were no lifeboats.) Apparently the course was so arranged as to preclude sight of anything of a naval nature. The Pacific arena might have been at peace (except for the lack of commercial shipping) as our *Teia*, like a lone swan, seemed to possess the pond. Yes, we shared experiences, strode the crowded deck, conducted popular lectures, group singing, and worship services to redeem the time; but also I found perpetual fascination in the surrounding natural world along with the joyous sense of movement. The expanse of the waters, the abounding ocean life, the unsurpassable glory of sunrise and sunset seemed to illuminate the mind and nourish the soul. As to food, it was tolerable and scant. Should the three small meals be rated as dull and inadequate, tea time offered a few luxury items as supplement: thin sandwich, slice of cake, an apple—all on a cash basis. A small store of potatoes under a tarpaulin on the foredeck, apparently not in good favor with the Japanese cooks, soon turned foul in the tropical sun and was cast overboard; but rice, the staple food, could also acquire its minor impurities. One of the Roman Catholic sisters, known for their forbearance, sweetly remarked, "I am getting a little tired of this diet of worms."

After twenty-five days of practically steady voyage we reached destination number one. This meant the little port of Mormugão, in the Portuguese neutral territory of Goa on the west coast of India, which had been marked for prisoner exchange. In the meantime our vessel had weighed anchor three times for taking on repatriates: Hong Kong added about fifty; Manila, a much larger number; and Saigon, just a few. She also stopped close to Singapore, in the open ocean, for taking on oil and water. While this former strategic area of the British Navy brought nothing of military significance to our view, it afforded some very interesting aspects of the natural world. Passing slowly through the Soenda Strait, we watched in the distance the fiery mouth of Krakatau Volcano, and through the night of October 4 we celebrated the starry splendor of equatorial midnight. Perhaps this also marked the frontier of Japanese primary concern, since passing into the Indian Ocean the *Teia* dropped her pilot ship.

On October 15, with a deep breath of relief and eager anticipations, we glided into the attractive and historically notable harbor of Portuguese Goa, two hundred miles south of Bombay. Presenting an array of rail tracks, freight cars, and great electric derricks for ship-loading—shades of peacetime when German ships daily carried off their rich cargo of teak logs and manganese—the port now stood utterly idle. Naturally, as we were still prisoners of Japan, no one was allowed ashore. We did rate it a privilege, however, to step down on the wharf and parade the length of the ship on neutral property. From the deck we beheld a view of rare scenic and historic importance. Before us stood a two-hundred-foot rocky plateau capped by an aged fort of brown-gray stone, a lower level presenting the Portuguese Ancient Palace with massive wall and great wood-iron gate bearing above it (as we were told) the venerated inscription "St. Francis Xavier 1620," and the shoreline offering magnificent banyan trees anchored to mother earth by their self-forged cables. Amid this natural grandeur one sensed the voices of history.

The next day the Swedish M.S. *Gripsholm* appeared! My heart gave a leap on seeing this great white swan adorned with blue and orange stripes on her bow and three golden crowns on each of her blue funnels. Surely this ship symbolized the hopes of humanity. Already, ours had become to us truly a "mercy ship" that merited much gratitude despite its inadequacies. Bow to stern we stood for three days awaiting the completion of exchange procedures and presenting the while a cool posture of uncongeniality. Fraternization was not in the books! The children, of course, assuming their natural liberties, called across to learn what there was to eat. *Gripsholm* announced: "For breakfast cornflakes and milk and for dinner turkey and ice cream." *Teia* responded: "Wormy rice gruel in the morning and curried meat chips with rice in the evening." In this uneven game, the dice had been cast strongly in our favor, a situation of which our Japanese friends probably were fully aware, having themselves come from an economy of relative abundance into one of harsh scarcity. Toward a balance, each was allowed to bring along thirty cubic feet of goods and three hundred dollars in U.S. currency. Prisoner exchange eventuated on the morning of October 20. I chanced to be among the first

hundred as two human streams flowed single file in opposite directions, being mathematically traded man for man.
In all, 3,002 repatriates, by this Red Cross transfer, were
being restored to the freedom and the service of our respective countries—among us 660 missionaries.

Could any of us have imagined such a bountiful reception as was presently offered by the *Gripsholm?* Accommodations and services seemed utterly overwhelming, as we
glimpsed vast decks, luxurious lounges, and ten long tables
loaded with Swedish smorgasbord of unbelievable variety
and abundance. It hardly seemed real—this earthly heaven.
But, filled with gratitude and the lust of living, I promptly
yielded to the necessity of social and gastronomic readjustments. From here on, our voyage would carry the spirit
and comforts of the homeland.

Remarks, running current, of having "exchanged a cross
for a crown" quickly became applicable in the deepest
sense. One of our voyagers entered the eternal. Our dear
household fellow, Hille Arthur, who had blessedly re-
gained strength and clarity on the *Teia* and in triumph accomplished the exchange, was called out of this life. Relaxing in an easy chair, he suddenly collapsed and then
died in the ship's hospital. This meant that the first days of
freedom occupied several of us with locally arranged memorial and burial services. In the tiny Anglican chapel on
the harbor cliff, our special group (ten closest friends) solemnly gathered, Edwin Walline officiating. How simple
and sacred the natural setting: plain casket overdraped
with the American flag, pulpit adorned with white lilies as
symbols of the resurrection hope, and at the open window
a cluster of rustic daisies gracefully attended by a teeter-
ing butterfly. The lonely burial took place in the small
Protestant cemetery about twenty miles out by automobile and ferry (*Life*'s photographers taking pictures).

Incidentally, this inshore trip afforded a slight acquaintance with the Goa area. Passing through the town of New
Goa, we caught interesting glimpses of Portuguese-style
architecture, native (Indian) habitats, and a variety of
tropical fruits. Old Goa, five miles beyond, had long lain
in ruins. Noted in the sixteenth century as the Portuguese
political and religious center of the East, it could boast in
this day only the great Franciscan Gothic cathedral (restored), which is significant for holding the sacred shrine
with the preserved body of St. Francis Xavier, early missionary in Goa.

Not until after leaving port, on the basis of accepted
regulations, was any news to be issued or mail to be delivered. Keen anxiety and tension prevailed these couple of
days. On the morning of October 22, outside the harbor,
the long night of darkness was finally broken as the windows, long shuttered against the family circle and the affairs of the world, began to swing open. If the restoration
of personal freedom be deemed the greatest blessing, is
not the resumption of communication a close second?

Eagerly, a cablegram is opened. It brings parental greeting; but, why is it signed "Mother"? The flash comes—Father is gone! Now comes to hand a letter from Grace and
the children. At long last, the year and a half of blank silence is ended. Immediately, I realize that numerous letters have been sent, many of them coming back and this
one of August 24 being just another venture of hope. The
Gripsholm, going out of New York, might get it on its way
to Shanghai, or, much better, I might really be returning
on the ship. The fact of my name not appearing on the lists
of repatriates was making the disappointment almost unbearable.

No word of any kind had come from me since October,

1942. Presently, I became aware, from this flash picture, that the burden of anxiety they must have been bearing was much more weighty than mine. The next day a letter from Stanton turned up, sent to the ship on the same supposition of reaching me some way or another. It brought general family information, especially sharing the solemn news of Father's death on May 8, after serious illness. I recalled with gratitude the special visit in the summer of 1940.

Eager to learn about the war, here we found access to the American news file from the war office (dated Oct. 11). South Pacific: "Allied land, sea and air forces getting into strategic positions; Europe: Advance in Italy—taking of Naples, and Red Army crossing the Dnieper R. to cut Germans off from the Crimea."

Life on the *Gripsholm* was fresh and rejuvenating. One began to feel a renewed identity with the life of the world. Once again, we enjoyed independence and privacy, comforts and plenty, gentility and romance, communication and enlightenment. We had changed worlds. Meals were not lavish but abundantly nourishing and supplemented with fruit drinks, chocolate bars, and vitamin pills. A dozen typewriters were available for use, stacks of relatively new magazines and daily news bulletins were at hand, and two evenings a week there was an entertaining motion picture. There were consultations with State Department officials and the filling out of their long questionnaire forms. The days passed quickly, including stimulating lectures and participation in musicals, worship services, missionary group plannings, and deck recreations. Dramatics of nature, on the generally smooth green-blue sea, offered the sportive maneuverings of sharks, porpoises, and spritely flying fish, with also the rare visits of the swift

frigate bird (man-of-war) and the lonely wandering alba-
tross. And, who could cease to be enamored and enriched
by the glory of ever-changing sunsets and the awesome
galaxies of the night!

Arrival on November 2 at Port Elizabeth (British), on
the southern extremity of Africa, reaped another bit of
mail; most important—an airgraph greeting from Grace
saying she would meet me in Montreal. There was a letter
also, dated September 28, telling of her wonderful surprise
and great relief after having practically given up all hopes
of my return. From Dr. L. S. Ruland, our China Secretary
at the Mission Board offices in New York, had just come a
note that changed her whole outlook on life. My being on
the *Gripsholm* was confirmed. But, strangely, the matter
was so shrouded in mystery as to forbid her sharing the
news with anyone for several weeks (probably on order
from the Canadian Government, due to my "political prisoner" status). This airmail letter, containing also chatty
notes from the daughters, had been forwarded by courtesy
of the American Consulate in New York. Now, at this
stage, the doors of communication began to be open both
ways, and I was enabled to send assuring airgraph messages to several strands of the family—saying, "Home for
Christmas."

Port Elizabeth brought us our first sight and touch of
Allied territory, and it seemed to be extending a brilliant
welcome from afar. In our late evening approach, the harbor presented a great semicircle of flashing greenish and
golden lights—an almost forgotten sight in areas of war.
Could it be a thousand torches of liberty into whose out-
stretched and encircling arms we were gliding! Then, under the morning sun, past an array of white buildings
draped neatly over the hillside of this tidy British port, a

greeting crowd kept moving toward us. What met us at the dock was a group of representatives of the British Armed Services, both men and women, offering us the freedom of the town; and on departure the thoughts we carried away were of warmth of friendship, luscious fruits, and bounty of flowers.

Next we headed for Brazil. This set for us a steady two weeks' run, around the notable Cape of Good Hope and directly across the expanse of the South Atlantic to Rio de Janeiro. What better time and opportunity to relax and rejuvenate? In preparation for that important stop and two-day visit we were given the benefit of a lecture on aspects of the country and people by Mr. Davis, U.S. Inspector of Consular Services in the Far East, who was also a repatriate, having been caught in Manila at the outbreak of the war.

Entering the great bay in the night of November 14 inspired no immediate enthusiasm. Only a dim glow showed up on the horizon, while closer by, out of the blackness (war precautions) a lighthouse blinked faithfully as though communicating with the luminous cluster overhead—the Southern Cross. In the morning, after the slow lifting of the fog, the sight became the more startling. A great city of rare beauty, edging the placid bay and surrounded by mountain ranges, lay before us, and our ship moving closely into the dock seemed to be losing itself among the tall, stately buildings.

Having debarked directly in front of the Touring Club of Brazil, I was almost immediately confronted by two smiling young ladies, one wearing a badge of Canada and the other labeled Presbyterian Church. Simultaneously I accepted the gracious greetings of both—just a beginning of the flood of glad hands and cordial invitations. The glamorous city, in special holiday mood since it was Brazilian Republican Day, seemed to be open for the taking.

Among the offerings of both consulates and churches were winter clothing for those in need, cash allowances (tentative) for shore expenditures, conducted tours in open tramcars to various parts of the city, and the special "Presbyterian Dinner" in the glittering new Y.M.C.A., where we enjoyed the fellowship of national church leaders and some talented entertainment. Also, a high point of experience was a half-day trip to Hunchback Mountain and Sugarloaf Peak, which afforded a panoramic view of the entire bay and city and brought us to the base of the unique statue of Christ the Redeemer.

A crop of radiograms and airmail letters brought me into contact with various family members and the Mission Board offices in New York, the most striking item being a letter from brother Earl, then in the Armed Services. I learned that he was chaplain to the Royal Canadian Air Force, ranking as squadron leader (major) and stationed in London, England. His duties included the intimate contact of being the last man to see the daring fliers on takeoff and the first to greet those that came back. He referred to Father's illness and concern for my welfare, one of his last questions being, "Do you think Roy will get out?" To this was a positive, "Yes." I felt deeply grateful for Earl's assurance. And, to a dear aunt's query, "How did you manage it?" I could only reply, "By the many trusting prayers."

From here on it was the last lap. Just fourteen days to New York seemed to me a very short time and distance. After all that lay behind, life on our ship was good, the sea our friend, the days not weary, and the goal almost in sight. I elaborated my diary, feasted on the latest journals, and rejoiced at the projected plans by American govern-

ment and church organizations for large-scale postwar rehabilitation. That word "rehabilitation" struck deep; it
raised a hopeful note against the dreadful years of devastation and death. Thanksgiving Day was celebrated on
November 25 by worship and feast and contributions,
eight hundred dollars being gathered up for the Red Cross.

On the morning of December 1 we hailed the Statue of
Liberty, ending our memorable seventy-three days of
ocean voyage. The Canadians, a party of 217, were the first
to leave ship. Without inspection or any other contact, we
were whisked by waiting busses to the Montreal-bound
train, which took us off in special coaches. (This spared
the U.S. all the trouble of clearings.) Then—finally—on the
Montreal station platform, Grace and I fell into each other's arms! A couple of days later I visited Mother in Kitchener and then had a look at Virginia and Mary Frances in
a hotel room at Windsor—and how they had grown! It required weeks to obtain police clearance from Ottawa, re-
lease of frozen bank accounts, etc., these being necessary
for the granting of a U.S. residence visa. December the
24th, three years to the day from our separation in Shanghai, we again became a united family.

While the girls were elated, Grace was quiet. I realized
that all attempts to get information had completely failed,
and only by pure accident had she gotten an inkling of my
situation. What became of the International Red Cross
letter I was permitted to send from camp last summer? It
was not utterly lost but a little late! Apparently having
been held in Tokyo (Japanese stamp, Oct. 2, 1943), it fell
into the hands of the American Red Cross Inquiry Unit on
Feb. 4, 1944, and was delivered to us in Ann Arbor by the
Mission Board on Feb. 15. In these war times, some letters
had similar or longer delays. The last one written to me by

Father, dated Sept. 7, 1942, and addressed to me in Shanghai "via *Gripsholm* steamer from New York," strangely turned up Feb. 5, 1945.

Not to be forgotten were the comrades remaining in the prison camp. Having stored in my mind the home addresses of several (no written word could be carried out), I immediately sent airgraph messages to their families in England, giving information regarding the "lost men" at Haiphong Road.

13

FRATERNAL WORKER

$\mathcal{T}$HE URGENT CALL from Hangchow for my return came in mid-1946. Our college (university), after nine years of refugee wanderings, had come back to the waiting Dragon Hills. Joyfully, I pictured the scene of awakening and resurrection, with President Lee and a small corps of associates vigorously undertaking the task. And I yearned to be one of them in this creative process of rehabilitating the campus and restoring the academic standards and dynamic spirit of our cherished institution.

Unfortunately, circumstances precluded my positive and immediate response. With residence in Ann Arbor, after a few months of adjusting myself to current American ways of thought and life, I had plunged into a season of deputation work (1944). This was designated by the Board as Furlough Fellowship Service, for the purpose of informing and inspiring the home church on the Christian outlook in Asia. It gave me wide and rewarding contacts with church groups, service clubs, schools, and youth camps. It also produced, incidentally, some incongruous situations, such as the occasion when the minister passed to me the whispered advice, "These are hardheaded businessmen; don't draw your punches." Since I had never heard the phrase on

punches, but well understood "don't," the effect proved
negative all around.

My next year offered the privilege of devoting myself to
research in political studies at the University of Chicago,
with residence in the International House, after which the
time would then have been suitable for return to China,
except for the factors of my health and the unresolved
problem of family adjustments.

As a temporary expedient I joined the staff of Adrian
College, Michigan, and our plan was definitely set for my
return to China a year hence. I would first go alone. This
led then to the family location's being shifted to Wooster,
Ohio, where Virginia entered college and Mary Frances
completed high school. The girls could thus have another
year of stable homelife and the benefit of their mother's
guidance, while I would test out the apparently harsh living conditions on the Hangchow campus.

I sailed from San Francisco in mid-August, 1947, finding
in the *Marine Lynx* a poor pretense of being an ocean liner,
and likewise Shanghai far from its old self. Obviously,
years would be required for recovery in both West and
East. The incalculable losses of war must fully arouse man-
kind to the will and the ways of "waging peace"! As I
caught up this sense of urgency I realized also a degree of
comfort in observing and sharing Shanghai's struggle for
renewal from the exhaustions of war.

Rather shabby and disorganized, the city had not restored its former smoothness and confidence in business
and administration. A typical experience came to me even
in the customs shed after debarking, where for two hours
I searched in vain for a missing suitcase containing my
daily essentials (recovered weeks later, some costly articles missing). Our Mission offices, upon which all of us depended so much, kept struggling daily with perplexing

monetary problems, official red tape, shipping delays, scarce missionary housing, and the like. Yet, thank God, Shanghai was carrying on.

Only after three weeks of wearisome bustling around did I manage to set my personal matters in order and get off to Hangchow. One example: merely getting an ordinary radio registered and released necessitated calls at numerous disconnected offices and handling more than a dozen business forms, so unbelievably cumbersome were the import regulations and processes.

And then, how about my scattered household effects? Five years had passed since these were given into the care of several friends—two Chinese families and one German. With sentimental relief and deep gratitude, I was able to locate and reclaim nearly all these items so faithfully kept in safety unto my return. But, having all such matters adjusted in good grace and getting articles reassembled and taken securely to Hangchow brought unimaginable hurdles and delays.

Naturally, I turned to the China Travel Service, long reputed for their reliability and efficiency. We concluded, instead of trusting to railway freight, which involved costly packing and handling risk, it would be better to assemble all on a truck and try the Shanghai-Hangchow motor road, myself accompanying.

That bright and brisk September morning the driver and I were in good spirits. Our load had been carefully arranged and secured, and then the clay-packed roadway proved to be not bad. Yes, this 150-mile drive through the countryside would be a pleasure and achievement; six to seven hours should do it, even with unforeseen delays. "Nice going," we said as we passed midway, and then—a sudden stop! What an incredible thing! In unbelief we gazed at the enormous gap in front of us (remains of wartime sabotage). With no possibility of crossing and no reconnecting detour, we were simply dead stuck. My Chinese trucker friend and I looked at each other in puzzlement—what to do now? The answer was simple: Each of us heaved a sigh, then together we had a good laugh (the joke on us); we dug out our packed lunch and ate; then, backing the truck to a spot where we could turn around, we glumly retreated to Shanghai.

Strangely, the China Travel Service had no awareness of this remaining wartime cut in the road, nor did the highway police stationed along the way bother to offer us any warning. Who was to blame and what result? The travel service and I each undertook to bear half of the cost for this abortive attempt and then had the goods shipped by railway freight after all. So, finally, with the blessing of having recovered basic household equipment and also books and typewriter, I felt prepared for my prospective bachelor-den living and resumption of professorial services.

President Lee had already greeted me at the dock. Now, the simple expression of warmth and general rejoicing at my actual arrival evoked in me a deep satisfaction. I felt the thrill of acceptance into the fellowship. Students and staff numbering over eight hundred, I became just another one among them, though the only non-Chinese in the College Hill community of a thousand.

A sensitive matter in my mind related to the long-presumed superior status of the missionary. It had ceased to apply. Our missions in China, especially educational institutions, had been reaching beyond this concept for decades, so that foreign and native leaders were marching shoulder to shoulder in the Lord's service corps. The time had come for one's status to be that of a *fraternal worker, called*, rather than a *missionary, sent*. This ideal, I felt, was now being actually achieved and the joy of it realized. A delightful experience confirmed it all: When I remarked to the dean (in former years my associate) that I would need a day to get settled, he promptly advised, "Please provide me with a written request that you may be officially excused and students properly informed."

However, one factor had immediately arisen that seemed to establish an ambiguous situation in our fraternal relationships. It pertained to housing. To my surprise, I was officially escorted to the only residence that had as yet been restored, completely renovated, within and without. "This house is prepared for the Mission worker," the president said, "and is entirely for you to occupy until others may come." Practically, it meant that in contrast to general staff housing—still in dilapidated buildings and crowded circumstances—I was being set up in a privileged position. But, what else could one do? With a mingled feeling of reluctance and gratitude I dutifully accepted the courtesy. Due to its prominent position on the hillside and the stately portico pillars (white), the students had dubbed it the White House.

My assigned courses, already delayed, began swinging into action. Largely, it meant stepping into unfilled gaps. First, I met a class of freshman English, numbering no fewer than fifty students, and followed with a packed room of eighty for modern European history. For effective handling, both groups were intended to be divided; but this was a step which had to await the arrival of more teaching help in the persons of Dr. and Mrs. Clarence B. Day, English language department, temporarily stationed in India and delayed by civil war. Obviously, English language instruction and drill presented the most urgent need. As my courses were taught through the medium of English, including both history and government, they opened possibilities of being doubly rewarding. The less wieldy group in sophomore English proved particularly enjoyable. Samplings of classical essays and selective bits of English and American poetry evoked sensitive response in their imaginative minds. Seemingly, whether majoring in engineering, commerce, or arts, the hearing of English spoken as a native tongue became an acceptable treat.

The imparting of knowledge may have its burdens, but the wellspring of eager minds makes them light. These young people were bent upon learning. In every class I spied familiar faces—younger brothers and sisters of former students. The girls (180 enrolled) impressed me as particularly alert and attractive, many of them having replaced their traditional gown with the new mode of white shirtwaist and formfitting overalls. And, as to a feminine vocation, it was hardly surprising to find the president's elder daughter majoring in architectural engineering and leading her class. Furthermore, such natural openheartedness and freedom from inhibitions as displayed by my students (such as the group's giving me a surprise visit and taking over the kitchen) gave assurance of oneness of spirit.

As to the physical aspects of the campus, now I was meeting at every turn the depressing scars of war. High up the slope I lingered long by a touching sight, the heap of rubble that remained of the longtime home of Arthur March, the biologist. The residences, especially those on the outskirts, had fallen victim, several being totally destroyed. Apparently, the whole set of main administrative buildings had suffered no basic structural damages and had already been given primary rehabilitation, but interior losses were tremendous. Upon recovery, all had been found totally despoiled of furnishings and equipment. Science Hall stood stripped; Alumni Library was left barren of books, shelves and all; while Tooker Chapel, a mere shell, had served as a stable for the horses. (Alas, that cherished little pipe organ!)

Restorations all around were vigorously in progress. Primarily, President Lee, Dean Ku, and Registrar Chen had undertaken the task of campus renewal and had rallied students to a reopening in the autumn of 1946. While still with many makeshift arrangements and genuine hardships, the institution had already achieved a worthy working system and a high quality of spirit.

Through the United Board for Christian Colleges in China (headquarters, New York) came an encouraging flow of material support; their contribution of $125,000 setting also a goal for similar aid from Chinese sources. Besides, several church colleges in the United States made generous donations, including such pressing essentials as shipments of double-decker beds, army-surplus blankets, and a sizable store of library books. So, Hangchow, as also other Mission-sponsored institutions, was regaining its position and fulfilling its function while at the same time anticipating its place in the projected union of the four East China area Christian universities.

Visits into the city brought me the happy realization that churches, Mission Hospital, Christian middle schools, had all sprung to new life again. And our Mission compound was literally buzzing with service projects for the needy, women making up garments from Red Cross supplies and the crowd of undernourished children coming in daily for that bowl of rich soup, followed by organized play and hymn singing (directed by Mrs. Van Evera).

Noticeably, in this area, so richly endowed with the symbols of native religions, monasteries and temples experienced revival and were presenting an aspect of renewal inside and out. To my inquiry as to source of funds, I got from a Chinese friend the quite brusque reply: "The fat-bellied merchants are rolling in dollars, so now are paying respect to the gods for wartime profits and postwar prosperity." At that moment, the Y.M.C.A. was holding its national conference on the close-by Taoist Temple Hill, and this was just one demonstration of how attractive temple and monastery establishments actually served various purposes not entirely unrelated to the challenging needs of contemporary society.

Truly, this hour in China was demanding of youth keen social and spiritual inquiry. How tragic that after long, exhaustive war the country had fallen again into civil strife! A flood of issues had to be faced: urgency of economic recovery, questions of political loyalty, rights of individual liberty, and the possession of a vital and working faith. In terms of ethical insights and the dynamics of living, none of these could stand beyond the concern of Christian education. One of the impressive aspects of the Chinese church, arising out of the strains of war, was the remarkable development of lay leadership and a spirit of stewardship, and the other was the awakened mind of youth.

Again the college church functioned as religious center. The Sunday worship service (voluntary) and weekday chapel exercises were, however, sometimes overshadowed by the lively fellowship groups. In the latter, many students and staff members were participating enthusiastically, combining fellowship, study, and prayer. Regular Bible instruction went on, both as curricular classes (elective) and other outside offerings. As to pastor, the pulpit was officially vacant (a need later met). Leading faculty members, taking turn, did most of the preaching. Actually, out of this vigorous lay leadership and common participation flowed a special zeal, producing a worthy standard of Christian worship. We had the urgent message of the basic evangelic gospel and also such challenging themes as "Gift of a Sound Mind" and "Christian Resources and Bearing the Cross." Surely, the fruits of Christian witness none can measure in numbers. Nevertheless, we rejoiced to find by the end of the year that thirty-six new disciples, including several staff members, had been added and many waiting inquirers were still under instruction.

The burdensome factor in our campus living, in many ways harsh, was the growing economic distress. Again, austerity became the familiar way of life. Having endured the makeshift years of warfare, surely better could be hoped for; but now mounting inflation and high cost of living dictated otherwise. Many sorts of goods were in decreasing supply due to unremedied economic disorganization, and salaried income was devoured by monetary inflation.

Even the Mission worker, supported from abroad, faced this personal problem. My Chinese associate promptly advised: "Don't keep cash on hand; better do a little hoarding." Immediately, I laid up a store of firewood and invested in several five-gallon tins of gasoline—commodities of premium value. The ratio of exchange for a U.S. dollar into Chinese National Currency, which was long stabilized at a three-for-one rate, had by now ascended to a fleeting forty thousand to one. At the same time, a long-standing Mission agreement with the Government required paying our allowances only in CNC, which thus restricted freedom of monetary adjustments. The practical plan devised by our general treasurer was to reimburse each one of us for actual living expenses and then add the equivalent of forty-five U.S. dollars at mid-month exchange rate. But, with inflation constantly doubling month after month, we kept falling seriously behind.

In this predicament I found a new avenue. It was storing up tinned army-surplus food supplies. A real blessing it proved, to discover that such were still available in the city and handled by curbside street hawkers. Apart from quick means of spending evaporating cash, other values accrued. Shifting from strictly Chinese food as planned and secured by my cook (chiefly boiled rice, beans, and a bit of pork or fish), I swung into a richer and daintier diet. Imagine such delicacies as tropical butter (army spread), cheese, packed ham (Rath), mincemeat, powdered ice-cream mix, and chocolate pudding! Such imported goods in fresh condition, had they been available, would have cost ten times the price.

While austerity prevailed as a general condition, obviously my personal situation offered advantages. How I wished it might be shared with fellow workers. Most unbelievably, by spring of 1948 inflation had skyrocketed into the millions, reaching 3,000,000 at official rate (6,000,000 on the black market). How could the institution be financed and staff families supported? In fact, for a time most shops closed their doors or merely exposed empty shelves. We lived through a season of panic.

Mission institutions, particularly, suffered dire effects. On the one hand, student fees, unless paid in rice, brought little return, while on the other, Mission subsidies being exchanged at official rate carried only 50 percent purchasing value. Not only had current salaries fallen (general situation) to less than 40 percent of prewar scale, but also, in our case at least, the special "personnel survival fund" from abroad (eight thousand U.S. dollars) had become exhausted. In such impoverished straits, just how could these devoted Christian workers maintain themselves? I realized the full extremity when the engineering department head confided to me that his pay, in terms of real purchasing power, had been running about twenty-five U.S. dollars a month. More distressful was the experience of the librarian. It required half of the month's income to provide each of his three children with a pair of rubber shoes. To these good friends the whole money business was little more than a disastrous game of handling worthless millions.

Our major academic concerns centered on raising standards of educational efficiency. In the background, hectic war years had left their legacy of inferior basic preparation, while also Chinese higher education tended to function as a "spoon-fed grade factory." A Christian institution, we felt, must do for the student something much better.

When at midyear it became apparent that about 10 percent of the engineering students had substandard ratings and were about to fail their courses, the administration faced the crisis. A host of questions loomed: Misfits in department? Transfers to what? Benefit of tutoring? Matter of health, financial stress, or perhaps family troubles? Precisely, just how could we help? At a marathon faculty session (eight hours, with time out for a fellowship meal) fully a hundred individual cases from all departments were dealt with. To me it became a revealing and reassuring experience. Never had I witnessed such sustained patience and resourceful insights as were applied to the exploration and remedy of each case. The president held steadily to the heart of the matter—the student's personal development.

In reference to the problem of resurgent student unrest, our situation was holding remarkably steady. Politically, an increasingly chaotic condition obtained. Early in 1948 the Nationalist-Communist civil war, pressing down from Manchuria to North China, began to throw the entire

Yangtze Valley into apprehension. Hence, the student mind, contending with issues of opposing ideologies and conflicting loyalties, took on an explosive mood—especially so in Government universities. Alarmed, the Ministry of Education in Nanking issued sharp warning: "Settle down, or universities will be closed." At the same time, one became aware of repressive actions falling upon outspoken intellectuals and of numerous students' being arrested. Then, also, a rather critical incident of a year ago came to my ear. It was the matter of two of our students' having been summarily dismissed on grounds of subversive influence and trying to set up Communist cells. Certainly the Christian institution had to avoid such a trap as harboring revolutionary activity and thereby subjecting our academic sanctum to police raids.

In my estimation, President Lee communicated a strong sense of both Christian and civic responsibility, and he was no doubt justified in claiming that our students had a finer spirit and superior self-discipline than those in most other schools. What we further needed, he urged, was a strong course in the meaning of citizenship—and he wished my associate and I would proceed to set one up. An incident that particularly impressed me related to a Sunday morning service. A considerable body of the student fellowships decided to skip off and hold their separate worship on the hilltop, a pranklike breach to which several of us made protest. But the president viewed it calmly. Gentle, fatherly advice readily achieved the abandonment of this disruptive plan. As an elder, he explained to the church session that "these students have very good intentions, but simply don't realize their responsibilities as Christians and church members. They have been taught only evangelism, but very little about the corporate responsibilities of the Christian life." Then, on the following Sunday afternoon,

all of us participated in a well-planned and fully cooperative hilltop retreat.

Apart from the absorbing campus interests, there kept
coming to me renewals of cherished friendships. Almost
immediately, along came the smiling farmer Chu. His hail-
ing welcome sounded a very different note from that woeful parting ten years back ("Ah, ya, we shall all be dead").
What a joy to see him so alive and apparently prospering.
From his famed Dragon Well Tea Gardens he brought me
a package as his gift of remembrance.

At the city Y.M.C.A. I found surprise. Being greeted by
the educational secretary, I began to recall the features of
one of my fellowship boys in Shanghai—a lad of promise.
Out we went for a little Chinese feast together and to fill
in the gap of years. "Besides being my honored teacher, I
have come to regard you as my spiritual father" (the Chinese traditional respect for a teacher). "While brought up
in a Buddhist family, it is out of the Christian middle
school and college that I have gained my faith and life
purpose." Adding then, "It was the personality and the
acts, rather than preachments, that gave the message." Apparently, simple acts of concern and kindness, in times of
discouragement and need, had led this orphan boy to the
great decision. Instead of "empty Buddhism" he had seen
a religion of compassionate spirit and found a vital, working faith.

In Shanghai, accidentally, I found myself confronted
with an unforgettable face. It had been lost for many
years. This same cheerful and hardy Korean friend had
been one of our beloved students more than twenty years
before and was always remembered as a fine scholar, superior athlete, and devoted Christian. Some years later he
had suddenly appeared at our door in a state of extremity
and seeking seclusion. The trouble? He belonged to a Ko-

rean Nationalist secret group in Shanghai, and by cast of
lot had been required to throw a bomb at a visiting Japanese general—the injury not being fatal and the perpe-
trator not discovered. After a few days he left and was no
more heard of. Now, here we were meeting again, after all
these eventful years! "Oh, yes, I have endured much," he
admitted. "I was taken to the Bridge House repeatedly
and remained there for many months."

By way of broad contacts, it was good to realize that
Hangchow was again able to open its doors to the world.
For purposes of social, cultural, and religious association,
the "Garden City" attracted global attention as a gathering
place for international groups. First came the International
Y.W.C.A. meeting (October, 1947). Here I was privileged
to meet distinguished leaders from abroad, holding conference at the Lakeview Hotel—the veteran, Miss Emma
Kaufman, as aforementioned (Kitchener, Toronto, Tokyo), doing me the honors. Then, however, most regrettably the anticipated assembling of the International Missionary Council could not be realized, as political and military tensions became too alarming. To Hangchow also fell
the honor of hosting the regional Rotary International
(April, 1949), a function more limited in scale. The special
meaning of this group to us was their visit to our campus
and the holding of official worship service in our college
chapel.

Contacts of most vital concern came with the emergency
conference on National Christian Education (July, 1948).
Meeting on the Shanghai University campus, an assembly
of educators representing nearly all of China's thirteen
(Protestant) Christian universities grappled with the crucial issues of the moment. We faced many imponderables
and found few answers. Our deep fellowship brought rich

rewards, but all the agonizing searchings could not penetrate the clouds of political uncertainty: here was the whole people of China yearning for peace and economic recovery, but civil war was raging! The appalling prospect was that of a divided country—north of the Yangtze all turning Communist and the rest remaining Nationalist. If only a new statesman would arise, possessing the wisdom and power to direct a traditional "middle course." Would not all China bow at his feet? Can Christian institutions hope for survival under a Communist regime? How can we best redeem the time? Ten days of deliberation and planning (with also the support of the vice-minister of education, a staunch Christian) at least helped to bring a new focus to our mission in higher education, a resolve to persevere with all our resources and a readiness to trust to divine guidance. As to our particular attitude, relating to the Hangchow situation we sustained a note of optimism. The present status, it appeared, could be counted on for another year; furthermore, there arose a general belief that a Communist system when applied to the whole of China would of necessity be of moderate type.

Again, autumn semester of 1948 appeared to open strong and with promise. Progressive rehabilitation, new up-to-date equipment and increased personnel gave us such a high rating as to attract student applications up to nearly three thousand, while only three hundred freshmen could be admitted. As to my personal role, summer recess had occupied me mainly with supervising major repairs of three Mission residences and in other ways facilitating Mission-University cooperation. Political science instruction again fully resumed and, with a new Chinese associate added, I now devoted myself largely to upperclassmen, directing studies in the history of European diplomacy, recent political theory, and principles of public administration. At the same time I shared some duties connected with institutional finance.

Already, much earlier, my situation had greatly changed. For the previous spring semester the arrival of Dr. and Mrs. Day at the end of December had brought manifold relief to the campus. Their both doing full-time teaching in English language and literature gave a great boost to the academic program. Meanwhile, my domestic arrangements were markedly enhanced, as the forming of a united household stood all to my advantage. But, regrettably, I had been lax in foresight. By myself, habitually taking it in the rough, the sudden blast of winter had caught me with meager heating facilities. And, alas, the kitchen remained sadly unequipped—a grim welcome to the incoming hostess! Nevertheless, I began to enjoy real household management with amenities of the feminine touch.

Now, finally, late September, 1948, brought Grace on the scene. Again we set up our own establishment in the house formerly known as ours and regarded as home. In spite of every effort to have repairs and renovation completed for the reception, still hammer and saw were at it, finishing closets and cupboards (fortunately, not yet hammer and sickle). And then, before her freight came through bringing household necessities, our abode was already turned into a hostess house.

Emergencies sprang up all around, and almost immediately two families joined us. Fellow missioners, a Cheeloo University professor with wife and child moving from Shantung with their arts college, were in dire need of a home. Escaping Communist control, this institution was setting up refugee quarters in a Buddhist monastery close by. Then, out of the blue, dropped in a Fulbright Fellowship representative and wife (from Washington University, Seattle) to remain a few months on our campus. Affording these friends accommodations and services meant a packed house and a busy kitchen, a taxing task for a hostess lacking modern facilities and depending upon unskilled help. Furthermore, to us fell the privilege of keeping open house for a stream of callers to the campus. (Among these were the U.S. Consul General and his wife, from Shanghai, and Dr. and Mrs. Sherwood Eddy, on the last of their numerous tours in China.) All this homemaking and entertaining caught Grace unawares. She had fully anticipated devoting herself to teaching and student activities.

These days of campus life, nevertheless, marked precious times in the ever-deepening spirit of fraternalism. Seldom in over twenty-five years of congenial association had we experienced such enriching Christian fellowship and meaningful sense of racial identity. Was it a mutual striding toward Christian and cultural maturity? To know and to appreciate, to care and to share, seem to give expression to the values of life—whether the civilization be West or East. Here was so much to esteem in Chinese traditional culture and so much to be learned and to be emulated in their naturally ingrained art of living! Native simplicity, reasonableness, and forbearance often put to shame our rigid concepts and hasty judgments. Yet we commonly agreed that Chinese humanistic ethics also stood in need of a truly redemptive faith. Our Chinese brethren, no less than we, were drawing their spiritual illumination and activation from the redemptive love of Christ.

A magnificent ancient scroll now graced our living room wall. It held a twofold meaning. This piece of Chinese art, so exquisite in design and mellowed with age, presented a great cluster of peonies, traditionally ranked as the "king of flowers." They spoke of dignity and virtue; but they also spoke of love. The scroll, having come from the treasure store of a once Mandarin family, was given to me by a student in my Bible class.

Our home, so centrally set (just above the chapel), seemed to bring us closely within the circle of student interest and easy relationships. Well, almost anything could turn up. Now, the lady of the house, mounting the path after her class session, finds the front room appropriated for a singing rehearsal or, perchance, is greeted by the din of instrumental practice. While we are having lunch, an informal prayer group has quietly gathered for devotions under our welcoming camphor tree. Again, a pair of Christian Association representatives just drop in to borrow recordings of hymns and classical selections to broadcast cheer and inspiration from the gateway tower. Now, here comes David, newly graduated and already assigned by the church to serve at our off-campus Evangelistic and Social Service Center. Of reticent disposition and fully dedicated, he comes seeking our counsel and prayers. These all keep giving us a sense of belonging.

The Chinese love of festivity is something contagious. Theirs is also a genius for the art of celebration, the memorable occasion that we shared being the president's sixtieth birthday. Nearly two hundred personal friends and alumni members gathered to shower high esteem with eloquent words and an array of festive scrolls lettered in crimson and gilt. To the blessing of attaining sixty years was added the honor of his being chosen the first Chinese president of Hangchow College and having served devotedly and ably for twenty years. Compounding further this joyful event, to it was added also the celebration of Mr. and Mrs. Lee's twenty-fifth wedding anniversary. For us, personally, this homecoming also restored many associations of the past and bolstered fresh courage for the future. Then, how genuinely the day of honor and rejoicing concluded: lawn party over, wishes and gifts bestowed, and guests departed, a common staff dinner brought all our campus families together in community fellowship, closing with hymns of praise and prayers.

Obviously, the Lees, like many Chinese Christian lay leaders, lived by the principle and spirit that held achievement to be not a personal but a cooperative matter—a legacy of mission school training. Fresh and glorious in my mind stood that gracious act by which my return to the campus had been welcomed. It spoke of responsibility. It exemplified sacrificial brotherhood. The houses then occupied by the president, the dean, and others of the faculty were still in a state of disrepair (ceilings cracked, walls stained, and floors riddled by termites), but the helper from abroad must be served a trim and shining mansion! Did it not symbolize the new era? This new era would be one of distinctly Chinese initiative, coupled with full-hearted cooperation by churches abroad—a truly fraternal Christian enterprise.

Toward the end of November events became startling. Already Nanking stood under the Communist threat and the Yangtze Valley in peril. We could see that "unless the United States throws in her air force, the Nationalist Government holds hardly a chance." In quick order, official advice came for women with children and those of uncertain health to prepare for evacuation. Talk about "closing college" sprang up; students from South China rushed homeward. Ah, yes, a changeover might come in weeks! However, the emergency passed, and Hangchow University carried on.

While Nationalists were hoping desperately for American intervention, Chinese opinion appeared broadly divided as to the wisdom of thus further complicating the

civil war. We (Grace and I) could see no justification for
such a step nor promise of any long-range solution. On the
healthy background of century-long Sino-American goodwill, "Why now get ourselves involved in fighting the Chinese?" It appeared to us foolhardy; for surely the matters
of leadership, type of government, and social system were
exclusively for the Chinese to decide.

We also believed that East-West–sponsored Christian
enterprises should be kept in the fullest possible operation,
and at the same time we committed ourselves to the venture of trying to do missionary work under Chinese Communism.

14

EMBRACED BY LIBERATION

$\mathcal{A}$ FTERNOON, May 3, 1949, brought the New Order! Suddenly a unit of the People's Liberation Army sprang up among us and swept victoriously across the Dragon Hills. Communism, Chinese-brand, was now taking over. Just twelve days earlier, Nanking, capital of Nationalist China had fallen under the red banner, and three days ago Hangchow City—facing an army of ten thousand strong—had capitulated without resistance. But the campus situation, it seemed, always involved some special strategic factors. While being American-owned property, it was exposing a wooded area in elevated position, directly above the riverside highway and closely adjacent to the great bridge. Again, we were destined to catch the fireworks.

For two tense hours our establishment was caught in the midst of a raging battle. Very unexpectedly (contrary to official agreement), a machine-gun nest of Nationalist soldiers had lodged on the upper edge of the grounds and begun pouring their fire upon the advancing Communist troops. In reply, this raised all around us a storm of mortar and machine-gun blasts, one having been set up in our yard. Of course, on warning, precaution had been taken for everyone to remain closely and quietly indoors. Students

and Chinese staff families were all huddling on the floors
of the dormitories while we Mission workers kept secluded in our residences. Grace and I hugged the walls
between the windows. For some time, in this terrifying
and confused situation, one could not tell which army was
among us. Then, it really brought relief to us to catch a
glimpse of the red armbands. Peeping warily between the
curtains of an upstairs window, I spied that symbolic red
ribbon on the arm of each dashing soldier. Now the clash
would soon be over!

Here was the vanguard of our new masters. Remarkably,
no one suffered injury or molestation, as this disciplined
breed of soldiers swept through halls and houses, urging
calm and quiet while they searched the premises for hiding Nationalist soldiers. Our exciting two hours rated the
only military confrontation in Hangchow. The Nationalists, improperly appropriating our premises, were routed
out, a few being captured on the grounds and several killed
in flight down at the bridgehead.

After the past week of wearing uncertainties and appre-
hensive waiting night and day, the tension was finally broken. And, strangely enough, Grace and I had slept right
through that previous night while our Chinese associates
kept diligently on the watch—kindly not disclosing to us
their knowledge of the immediacy of Communist take-
over. Now a universal sense of relief pervaded the campus.
The military crisis over, we could again settle down to undisturbed studies—or, could we?

Once again, in the nearly three decades of our sojourn,
we were finding ourselves immersed in one of those recur-
ring upheavals of China's travail in the processes toward
modern self-realization. In 1927 it was the Nationalist Revolution, in 1937 the Japanese onslaught, and now the great
turning of the wheel by Socialist take-over. Each brought

its crop of crises and emergencies. Each grounded more deeply our sense of concern and identification.

Notably, the ten days immediately preceding "liberation" had furnished their share of excitement and anxieties. Everyone had to think of safety, of the probability of isolation, of food shortages, and of lack of funds—for who knows how long? Quickly, our responsibilities were somewhat relieved by suspension of classes, and over half of the students hurried home. However, emergency protection had to be organized for dealing with possible riots or other dangerous eventualities. Stores of food and medical supplies needed to be obtained and laid up, and reserve money resources had to be placed on hand. These were urgencies.

A Chinese associate and I had walked into the city (ten miles, round trip) to secure medical necessities at the Mission Hospital. The shops were closed and streets deserted, except that large bodies of soldiers, having appropriated all types of conveyances, were on the move. Here and there police squads and fire department units toured around. Hangchow was facing the crisis in an orderly manner. Having been shocked by the fighting and spoilation in Nanking and around Soochow, the Chamber of Commerce was determined to arrange a peaceful turnover.

Almost at the last minute, four of us undertook a special trip to Shanghai. Our pressing concern was the inadequacy of emergency funds; and these, due to serious inflation, were required to be strictly in the form of durable value. We also considered it a worthy venture to drive the new Chevrolet car to Shanghai in hopes of safekeeping there. (It had recently replaced our rickety war-surplus weapons carrier.) Two Chinese staff members and I, driven by the trusty chauffeur, managed to do the job, though just barely.

Proceeding on the Hangchow-Shanghai highway (which

had so disappointingly failed me in September, 1947) we fell into circumstantial good fortune. Not far out of the city, close to the airdrome, we somehow became mingled in a long line of trucks having obvious connection with the National Aviation School. They were evacuating to Taiwan. Now, surely these dignitaries in shining car and capped driver must be officials attending the train of trucks. So, apparently, thought the highway guards as they promptly waved us by at every check station. In the midst of these military tensions, we might readily have struck trouble. Reaching the western outskirts of Shanghai, we entered a heavily congested defense area, soldiers busily constructing barriers, and excited residents streaming into the city by the thousands. We had done well to cover the 150 miles in six hours. But from there it meant barely creeping along for two exhausting hours to reach the heart of Shanghai.

Directly, wild tales floated to our ears: the incredible speed of the Liberation Army, defenses crumbling swiftly along the railway—Shanghai next, or maybe Hangchow! Just spreading false reports, we thought. By clever tactics of small units appearing suddenly in unexpected places the Communists would be softening the ground by their wily war of nerves.

Our next day, Monday, buzzed with business. The university treasurer and I hastened between banks and offices, handling drafts, gold bars, and stacks of silver dollars. These funds had been credited to us from New York as emergency appropriations. We needed to make them immediately available, while at the same time holding them in a form fully safeguarding against depreciation. Obviously, credit in Chinese banknotes would be worthless. Placing a reserve in care of the Associated Missions Treasurers, we divided our hoard among the four of us for carrying safely to Hangchow, and to me fell the honor (responsibility) of caring for those packages of nuggets simply wrapped in coarse brown paper.

Now what were the chances for getting back home? Railway offered the only means, but lying directly within the line of attack, none could know as to "if and when." Early next morning we squatted at the Union Station. For several hours all appeared dead and hopeless—no movement on the tracks, no schedule posted, no ticket office open. Suddenly, a stir! and we dashed with the crowd for a spot in the coach. It was a start. There was a train and we were on, yet when would it go? Another four hours passed before it had nerve to creep cautiously and quietly out. From late afternoon, through the night until six in the morning, we rolled and we stopped, we dozed and we cramped in the squeeze, and without the flicker of a light or sound of a toot we journeyed safely to Hangchow. With thanks to the railwaymen and to the relief of those anxiously awaiting us, we landed back home with mission accomplished. A close shave this was, as this very day all communications were being cut.

The New Order, suddenly at hand, began to provoke a flood of conjecture. How rapid and how radical would be the changes? Would the pattern of higher education, especially Christian colleges, be enabled to carry on? According to the prevailing view of the hour, the new regime would most certainly be occupied with primary tasks: extending military occupation, administering large cities, and reconstructing economic life. A considerable time gap might reasonably be expected before the overhauling of cultural institutions began. Among our Chinese associates emerged opinions that Christian institutions would be allowed relative freedom for two or three years, while others optimistically suggested even five or ten.

Obviously, there was at work a strategy of good first impressions. As for military discipline, administrative efficiency, and official courtesy, the record appeared impressive and reassuring. The small unit of protective soldiers stationed on the campus, without causing inconvenience, could not be objectionable. We were quite on our own. So the feeling spread: Yes, after all, this is *Chinese* Communism. When the young daughters of President Lee fearfully queried, "Father, aren't you fleeing for your life?" he assured them of his personal confidence in the reasonableness and moderation of the new rulers.

Considering the very disturbed political conditions, our scholastic year of 1948–1949 had been, up through April, remarkably successful. We reached a peak enrollment—over a thousand including our Shanghai branch, at the same time attaining progressively attractive academic standards. Of course, there prevailed continuous financial strains due to the never-ending inflationary process. Nevertheless, with the military crisis in our area of China now passing, there was real hope for making up lost time and achieving an orderly finish.

Not until the "liberation" of Shanghai, several weeks later, did the campus actually come to life again. And, in fact, a considerable portion of the student body had fled to the still unconquered South. These would surely not return. One midday early in June there arose a great jubilation. With five packed busloads of students having arrived from Shanghai, we considered that the condition and mood for study had now been restored. But—was it a delusion?

Almost immediately came news about a Government Special Training School. This was being hastily set up in a Buddhist temple and notice sent to college seniors to report immediately. Thus, without finals, one hundred and fifty of our arts and commerce majors went off; while, on the other hand, engineering graduates were officially advised first to complete their technical studies. Without doubt, the matter was crucial. Job opening and placement would be depending entirely upon this new training. To the students it became clear that satisfactory completion of two months' intensive indoctrination offered the only open door for employment. Many felt it a shocking stroke.

Our administration did all we could to ease and facilitate their abrupt departure—even to granting permission to borrow metal bed frames newly arrived from the U.S.A. In a few days, hastily arranged graduating exercises were set up, for which our seniors obtained special leave for a half-day return to their alma mater. Those simple exercises throbbed with a world of meaning. Did they mark the severing of a golden link? Could the acquired knowledge on the campus, these familiar ways and the prevailing spirit, find fusion in the emerging new society? Acute emotions attended the last words of advice and encouragement offered by the deans, and intimate warmth permeated the farewell tea party with faculty and staff. Sharply, an era had closed.

The new system, quite obviously, was being custom-cut for youth. It caught them up into active participation and high enthusiasm by daily rallies, parades, and slogans. A period of ten days for introducing the New Democracy was declared by authorities as first priority for all students and teachers. Lengthy daily assemblies were loaded with Marxist principles, to be followed by group discussions for application to current issues. All of us read Mao Tse-tung's booklet, *The Fight for a New China.* (The English-language edition, prepared by William Foster, 1945, rated this as "the fullest exposition of the policies and program of Chinese democracy.") On the lighter side came a wave of song and dance. These gay peasant harvest songs, accompanied by folk dances, gave artistic and emotional expression to the New Freedom. And to the students fell the pleasant duty of spreading this spirit among the children of villagers and workmen.

When would curricular essentials find time or place? When at last they did, we faced a critical situation. The administrative structure and policies were confronted with demands by the student self-government: Tests must be abolished! Executive Council must be democratized! Reactionaries must be cleared out! Teachers' salaries must be lowered! In a manner we carried on amid grinding frictions and noisy mass assemblies; meantime, the bulletin boards were plastered with irresponsible criticisms and bitter accusations. Under such ugly circumstances and even dire threats, President Lee resigned and left the campus.

Could all this have been officially directed? We considered it was probably not, but, rather, the action of a few of our ambitious firebrands having taken the bit. Yet, presumably, the Bureau of Education, had they desired, might readily have curbed such demagogically run student mass meetings and suppressed the lashing criticisms against our "whole reactionary group."

As Mission workers (only four of us), none was singled out as giving offense. We simply shared the general condemnation. The fundamental principles of Christian education, as conceived by our University Board of Control (almost entirely Chinese), had of recent date been clearly stated. Positively, they declared that, for the schools to be maintained as Christian institutions, under no circumstances could any of these three essentials be sacrificed: *academic standard, administrative integrity,* and *Christian character.* Personally, in spite of stormy seasons, I held hopes and faith that workable adjustments could be realized for at least a tentative continuance of China's Christian colleges and universities. And, most reassuring, stood the fact of our religious program's suffering no interference. Worship services, Bible studies, and vigorous fellowship groups kept carrying on as freely as before.

Just about this time, a cable arrived (mails having been suspended) from the United Board of Christian Colleges, New York, requesting me to "explain the situation." To this, I felt able to give some assurances, such as: "No soldiers lodged on campus; university under Committee leadership; radical student activities faded out; semester's finals being given; religious program continuing undisturbed." Then, also: "By official advice, Christian institutions are expected to 'carry on.' Until the military phase of the Revolution is completed and the People's National Government is established, no basic educational reconstruction will be undertaken."

"Liberation!" What was this striking exclamation propounded to mean? It implied that a whole people, living under social limitations and oppressions sustained by tradition and fostered by corrupt government, were about to be released from their manifold bondage. In a more realistic sense, the term "Liberated Areas" had come into use with expanding Communist control in Northern China (both prior to and after Japanese surrender). As early as April, 1945, before the Seventh Congress of the Chinese Communist Party, Mao Tse-tung had stated his principles of freedom. After naming the conventional Western concepts, "speech, press, assembly, association, thinking, belief, and body," he significantly added, "In all China only the people of the Liberated Areas enjoy this freedom." What an accusation—and what a promise!

In my observation, Communist take-over first of all heralded *peace*. The masses of China were so deathly sick of

war and disorder that at this stage the acceptance of a
vigorous Communist regime appeared to offer the best
hope. "Yes," had said a keenly observant friend of mine,
"I believe our people are now ready to try it." Conspicu-
ously, with every advance of the People's Army came the
waving banners bearing high the "dove of peace."

Next to peace, the Liberation proclaimed *deliverance.*
There were, indeed, many bondages lying heavily upon
the body and soul of China. The Nationalist Government,
despite its worthy record of twenty years of stable rule,
comparative national unity, and many constructive
achievements, had come seriously short in meeting the
needs of the masses. Under the wartime Kuomintang rule,
intellectuals increasingly despaired of a truly liberalized
Government; and the agricultural countryside appealed in
vain for the long-promised land reform. There remained
also the burdens of exploitive foreign commercialism, of
domestic bureaucratic capitalism, and of oppressive merchant profiteering.

Again, the Liberation professed to be establishing *democracy.* Each newly organized provincial government described itself as the People's Democratic Republic. While
clearly under the leadership and direction of the Communist Party, the "people" were credited with being the base
of all structures and functions of society (for example,
we had People's Bank Notes). However, in this new society, to the term "people" there were attached certain pre-
scribed limitations. Shut out from common rights and priv-
ileges were three groups of society: landlords, bureaucratic
capitalists, and Kuomintang Party members. The New Democracy, then being hailed, clearly specified "democracy
among the people and dictatorship over the reactionaries."

Quite genuinely, Liberation also carried a wave of *idealism.* It presented, especially to youth, the vision of a

dreamed-for New Era now being really at hand—a thorough and rapid transformation of China in which they could play a leading role. Could anything be more thrilling and more challenging? Viewed historically (though very superficially), Sun Yat-sen's *trial* Republic (1912–1927) had barely touched the ground; Chiang Kai-shek's *elite* Nationalist Republic (1928–1949) had failed the masses and thus inevitably floundered; the new Democracy of the People's Democratic Republic was giving strong promise of fulfillment by its remarkable demonstration of vision, action, strength, honesty, and spirit of sacrifice.

A rare letter from one of my students impressed me deeply. He had disappeared from class several months previously; and it was whispered to me, "He has gone North," meaning he had entered the Revolutionary Training School in Peking. Due to his quiet disposition, I had hardly known him and especially had not been aware of his sensitivity and high-mindedness. Apart from his compliment, which credited me with being "faithful in teaching and lovely in treatment" (?) I deemed it to be an act of real courage to have written thus openly to his Western teacher. Recalling "what a paradise Hangchow University is," he contrasted the "poor conditions" of the Training School. Yet, obviously, he gloried in privations for the sake of his dreams.

This brought freshly to mind a student of the early twenties. Of an unusually brilliant mind and deep sincerity, he wore the simplest garments and concerned himself with activities bespeaking spiritual values. His heart was set on taking up the torch so untimely laid down by his deceased father (Confucian scholar and modern educator). With such aspirations and the influences of our campus environment, quite naturally, he took up the Christian faith as

an acceptable and effective way of life. Then, after graduation he entered teaching, particularly stressing the new
critical approach to Chinese literature and history. Years
later, he seemed to us a sort of mystery man, vanishing
from the scene for months at a time. One day in the late
thirties he favored his teachers by coming into our home
and confidentially opening to us his very soul. Said he,
"Christianity is a good religion and a good teaching for
China; but it works too slowly. China can't wait!" Obviously, he had committed himself to the need of a thor-
oughgoing social revolution—and no more waiting! So,
during the coming years many able Chinese Christian leaders, especially Y.M.C.A. secretaries, became deeply disturbed by Christianity's too-feeble efforts at grappling
with social ills, and began noting, in contrast, Communism's dynamic program and actions.

15

UNWELCOME GUESTS

O CTOBER 2, 1949, launched a significant new landmark in China's history. With us, a solemn, ceremonial flag-raising opened our day. Across the far reaches of the land there was being celebrated the inauguration of the Central People's Government in Peking. The military phase of the Revolution was completed. Consolidation had begun. Already, through the years, first the varicolored five-bar flag of the Republic had waved over us; then came the banner of the Nationalist era with its white sun on blue and red. Now respect was due the new standard with brilliant red base and a cluster of five gold stars (one large and four small), symbolizing regional unity within a totally socialized system of society. How durable would this regime be? Three days of holiday ensued, mass demonstrations and parades taking over the life of our provincial capital. Rather uniquely, the engineering students expressed the spirit of a Christian university by constructing out of bamboo a beautifully designed bridge for their display. This symbol of peace and cooperation moved along among the harsh slogans proclaiming the "might of the people for smashing the enemies."

For fully a year the university continued to carry on,

lacking the leadership and stabilizing influence of a president. The large, democratically constituted Administrative Council included student representation to the extent
of three regular members plus three auditors. The Executive Committee of five bore the brunt of student self-government criticisms and interferences. In such day to day
maneuverings and hassles the processes of democracy were
being tried out and painfully learned.

In late autumn the University became subjected to an
exhaustive investigation by a special official from the Bureau of Education. After several weeks of observation and
probings, always with courtesy, he appeared satisfied with
what he found. We were, of course, duly pleased to be
found meriting a favorable report. Earlier I had faced the
problem of my political science studies. I was projecting
three courses to upper classmen: comparative political
systems, recent political thought, and world organization.
On submitting to the Bureau my outlines of study along
with titles of texts and reference books, the reply came:
"Go ahead. It is not what we want, but we are not ready.
Your method is considered objective." However, almost
immediately, revisions had to be applied to studies of history—especially pertaining to China, the Communist theory being that only by revolutions has social progress been
achieved.

Nothing, so far, had clarified our status as foreigners in
new China. It appeared that being already there placed us
naturally into the category of alien residents. Could we
also, as before in our type of services, be rated as honorable guests? First came registration with the Public Safety
Bureau. Far from being a matter of simply filling a form, it
involved an hour or more of personal interview, delving
into family background and many aspects of one's private
life and attitudes. After covering education, financial re-

sources, organizational connections, a prime question was, "Why did you come to China?" Since both Grace and I had been reared on the farm, engaged in common labor, and then also earned our way in obtaining higher education, we apparently were absolved from connection with the evils of wealth and exploitation of others. Our very modest Mission allowance also spoke for itself. We explained that our coming to China was by personal choice (though supported by the church) for the purpose of helping Chinese youth get a modern education. Conveniently, I considered (under the circumstances) my connections with International Rotary and Institute of Pacific Relations as automatically lapsed. (They had.) And having had no association with the Nationalist Government either in West China or recently in Taiwan, obviously I was politically quite unattached. Residential certificates were then forthcoming.

Shortly there arose the matter of foreigners wishing to leave. While Shanghai, as a port, had been closed for several months by Nationalist blockade, repatriation arrangements were nevertheless anticipated. At the same time doubts arose whether business personnel would be allowed to leave (suddenly disrupting the economy) and, on the other hand, whether missionaries would be permitted to stay. By late September all seemed clear, many Americans having left, including Mrs. Day, who judiciously returned to the U.S.A. rather than face the oncoming strains.

The residence certificates, which established legal status, brought corresponding restrictions. We lost our accustomed freedom of movement—actually not a discriminatory regulation, since it applied to everyone. The police needed to know at all times of every person's whereabouts. Leaving the campus required signing up and indicating where one was going; should we remain in the city over-

night, our presence as guests would be immediately reported by the host. Traveling any farther distance necessitated a special pass. The Student Union also issued to us a
certificate of residence and kept a strict watch on our
whereabouts.

Living conditions and costs were presenting no drastic
change. The introduction of a new currency, in People's
Bank Notes, which appeared at first to halt inflation, produced no miracles. By September, for example, the price of
rice had mounted threefold. One needed to concede that
an important factor may have been the Socialist policy of
more equitable distribution, which necessitated shipping
out products into areas of real distress. Quite naturally, local complaints of food shortages and high costs were given
the official squelch: "We know that Chekiang is a lush
province. At least twenty varieties of edible grasses are
growing here. You will never suffer starvation."

For handling our own household economy, we could still
rely on some remnants of war-surplus supplies, which re-
gardless of quality and age yet remained a real boon.
Probably the most unique item was the sixty pounds of
ground coffee preserved in a gunnysack (salvaged from a
hospital ship). Our share of twenty pounds embellished
many a breakfast—imagination taking over where flavor
failed. Our monthly stipend from the Mission (as we had
officially reported) amounted to fifty U.S. dollars each. It
was set thus, in accordance with our wish, to approximate
the scale of our Chinese co-workers.

Although we seldom left the grounds, we did not lack
the favor of visitors. Frequently and unannounced appeared a small band of off-duty soldiers, led by sheer curiosity. Having come from rural areas of distant provinces
they had occasion to wonder: What do these foreigners
look like and how do they live? Commonly, at our lunch-

time, grinning faces, sometimes as many as twenty, appeared at the veranda windows. Once they asked to come inside and watch us eat. That was granted. Seldom anything unpleasant occurred. Continually our place served somewhat as hostess house: From the congested city came our missionary friends to share the mountain breeze and chat over a cup of tea; former students from hither and yon dropped in to bring greetings; prominent Chinese visitors to the campus were ushered to our door.

But for two refreshing diversions, the summer of 1950 might have left us lonely and languishing in the heat. In July the East China Synod's youth conference assembled on the campus. The University being, as then, under the control of the Church of Christ in China, location and facilities proved most appropriate. Mingling with these 150 select young people so enthusiastically engaging in Christian studies and activities truly thrilled our hearts.

Then, remarkably, August afforded us a ten-day visit to Shanghai. From Mission headquarters in New York had come a little windfall of twenty-five dollars each, to be used for some refreshing change—getting off to a resort for a week or even securing up-to-date reading matter. We ventured for Shanghai and managed to obtain passes, Grace really having need for special optometrist services and I having University finances requiring attention. Nevertheless we made it a holiday! Visiting many friends and being lured to familiar places gave us just the lift we hoped for. The Community Church, which we had known so well, carried on a full program with large attendance—mainly Chinese. Downtown seemed to say, "Business as usual," showing little outward evidence of radical administrative changes. So, how about a season of self-indulgence? It appeared to suit the occasion. Besides the bountiful meals enjoyed at the tables of our friends, like honeybees we sampled the fares of noted restaurants. "Have you ever tried a planked steak at the Chocolate Shop?" a friend had asked. "But, oh, you must." The Chocolate Shop being a longtime favorite, we took the plunge, hoping at the same time that no acquaintance would spot us indulging in such extravagance. When that elaborate serving faced us (really on a plank with gravy ditch and all), we felt shocked at our undertaking such a feast, fully ample for several. Then friends appeared at our table to our embarrassment! At least our Shanghai holiday had netted a "once in a lifetime" splurge.

Again, school opening of autumn, 1950, came with an unexpected boom. With an enrollment of 900 regulars and 220 in the preparatory department, residence halls were bursting to the point of having dormitories opened in the attics. Most significant, the university board had by then appointed a highly rated president. Hope and confidence reigned afresh on the campus.

Certainly to us, as Mission personnel, the remarkable qualifications of our chief brought all for which we had been hoping and praying. Here, indeed, was the man for the task. From a South China family of modest material substance and social position, he had risen to a brilliant and influential career. Somehow finding means to achieve his aspirations, he studied in America, traveled in Europe, served in his government, presided for more than a decade over a leading university, and participated vitally in the National Christian Council. With the appointment of a man of such a wealth of experience, prestige, versatility, and singular insight, Hangchow University attained a new stature.

To us, personally, the greatest boon was the president's joining our household (of course including Clarence Day). Happily, such arrangement served a multiple purpose. To him (a single man) it could afford the amenities of family living, while fitting also into his broad outlook of harmonizing East and West. As for us, we were gaining invaluable enrichment and enlightenment by his congenial personality and sensitive grasp of every shifting situation.

Then, in November, came the fulfillment of another dream. Our search for a pastor and religious director was at last superbly rewarded. From study abroad returned this young theologian, neatly adapted to our campus needs and opportunities, and with him his well-trained wife to handle the finest church music. New ideas and new zeal began to energize the religious program, drawing intensive interest and adding a flood of baptisms (over forty in the school year). Peter also carried executive duties in the synod.

Thanksgiving Day, somehow, became especially meaningful. Sharpened by the tension of the times, autumn glories seemed never to have been so abounding or so poignant with spiritual significance. Personally, we felt our sense of gratitude reaching out to encompass all past and recent years on the Dragon Hills. Was it a new wave of assurance that truly the gospel and Christian way of life had here taken deep root in a multitude of hearts?

At the same time we were experiencing the ever-present strains of numerous depressives. The distressing poverty of so many students struggling to meet fee requirements and interference with regular studies by increased pressures of indoctrination kept grinding heavily. General nervousness pertaining to shocking family circumstances within the changing order also prevailed. First steps in the heralded land reform had by now gotten under way; and to numerous students this became an acute personal problem, as fathers or relatives were not only dispossessed but sometimes dealt harsh penalty for presumed past oppressions.

Most alarming and tragic was the mounting Korean war crisis. Rapidly it became the crucial factor in determining not merely the status of Americans still in China but the entire future of Sino-American relationships. With the entry of Chinese "volunteers" into North Korea, at once we had become enemies! The long record of friendship between the two great countries, East and West, was shattered. The United States, now condemned as the defender of imperialism, rated positively as the chief enemy of the Chinese people.

As for myself, it was hard to believe that such a calamitous situation could ever arise. So much had we loved China, so long felt at home, that I had persisted in the hope that some understanding and peaceful relationship might be worked out between Washington and Peking. However, the signals had already been given. I recalled how in October, 1949, the People's Central Government had sent out bids for recognition. To this expectation Soviet Russia responded quickly, Great Britain made a favorable gesture, but the United States kept blankly silent. Action by Congress had just been reported, as allocating 75 million dollars for military aid in the general area of China (Taiwan?).

Clearly, our days in China were now numbered. The question was: When? Not being either officially ordered out or directly subjected to criticism (though sensing a degree of isolation), we continued to regard ourselves as acceptable residents. Of this, intimate friends assured us. Then, one evening on the dark riverside road, the signal came. Grace and I, returning home from the Zakow railway station, became aware of a great company of our students marching ahead of us. Coming back from a red-hot rally in the city, they kept carrying on with the songs and slogans. "Listen! What are we hearing?"

On and on it went: "Hate the Americans! Kill the Americans!" We got the call, loud and clear. As we had once been called to service in China, we were now being called to leave. Not that we really feared for personal safety, but simply—our days of usefulness in China had ended. From now on, our presence would become an increasing burden and hazard to our deeply concerned Chinese associates and friends.

From this point on, we proceeded with applications for leaving the country. To our surprise, came the question, "Why?" What answer, with due courtesy, could guests of long residence offer? So, Grace, having become arthritic, put it squarely on the matter of health, while I referred to the urgency of caring for my aging mother. With applications in, packing began. We counted on getting off in about a month or six weeks, but time dragged on from November until early March. No word came. "Are they holding us?"

When finally the awaited notification arrived, it carried less the meaning of a permit than that of an order: "Day after tomorrow you shall leave for Shanghai." That moment, unhappily, caught me in bed under heavy attacks of malaria. Our plea gained us one day's extension.

Preparing to leave our long-established post cast up many moods and perplexities. Under the constant strain of delicate circumstances, our contacts, attitudes, and crucial decisions seemed to stand ever in the balance—though also blessedly eased by the ready counsel and unfailing assistance of a few "close standbys."

Household furnishings (sale not being permitted even if we had desired) were simply given away or left standing as part of residence equipment. Even our treasured antique peony scroll kept its place on the wall; it most surely would have taken flight at the first customs inspection.

Personal effects we could take along. In this case, general instructions set also the requirement of a specific manner of packing whereby *every* variety and quantity of items had to be listed and particular location in trunk designated (six duplicate copies required!).

Uncertainty about customs clearance of books and papers touched off exploration into the parcel-post situation. I was well rewarded. Very accommodatingly the businesslike postal clerk accepted my package as addressed to our Mission office in Hong Kong. He took my word as to contents and readily handled the matter. Gradually, by this route, a series of packages was dispatched, several different addresses in Hong Kong being used. So thus, a group of important documents and papers, a selection of family photos, and a small stock of prized books were started on the way.

Furthermore, one had to deal with questionable records. More and more we realized that connections with the West, especially the United States, placed people in dangerous positions. Historical sources became grist for purging the poison of "cultural imperialism." Records could so easily be misinterpreted, laying grounds for accusation and bringing dire penalties upon our Chinese brethren. How could we safeguard? Financial matters were held particularly crucial; and in this respect I had served as the link between the university and New York offices. The responsibility being mine, all related correspondence was promptly fed to the flames. Similarly, at the last meeting of the Hangchow Missionary Association such a question arose. Should these records covering more than fifty years be preserved? In the face of severe investigations, might not even these be used to evil purpose? Then, in well-chosen words the chairman announced our decision: "Will the secretary please carefully record this item in the minutes and forthwith burn the entire lot."

Wonderfully, in the midst of the strains of packing and breaking up our household came the glorious Christmastide. The spirit of it swept the campus. It seemed to say: "Only one day off; let us fill the measure to the brim. For this is the birthday of our Lord!" Perhaps of all times when Christian faith, goodwill, and joy reached heights of expression among us, Christmas of 1950 touched the peak.

In the bay window of the hostess house stood the shapely Christmas tree, candlelit and star-crowned, and round about hung huge bunches of brilliant holly. Christmas had opened with the sacred concert in the chapel, and now the thirty choir members were gathering merrily around our festive tables. The joyous celebration proceeded. From twelve to two o'clock in the starry night was the time set apart for the carolers, five student fellowships going the rounds by separate groups. Our household, joined by the pastor's family, stood in waiting. Now came floating midnight voices—"Silent night! Holy night!" As we opened wide the doors, "Noel! Noel!" came flooding in. Group after group came streaming through the house in devout merrymaking, each person accepting a little token gift—an orange, a cookie, or a bit of candy. Of such Holy Night visitors more than 150 passed through our home.

They told us of each fellowship's having a special room decorated and program prepared to carry on until morning. As for ourselves, before we could reach breakfast, rappings at the door brought shouts of "Merry Christmas" from numerous members of the staff. Then, city friends having joined us for the festal dinner, the celebration closed with a mass evening assemblage—all marching in the annual candlelight service.

To me this all seemed to match clearly the immediate

ideal and spirit of the university: What we do and while
we can, let us do it well; the days for free Christian witness
may not be long! And yet, how convincing was Communist atheism? An incident at the presbytery meeting in
the city shed some light. Letters were read from rural pastors stating that land reform had begun, chapels had been
taken over, and they themselves had become involved.
They ended with the plea, "Remember us by your prayers."
Promptly, a public safety observer confiscated these letters. In alarm, he asked, "Are you people here going to
pray that God will curse our land reform?"

Finally, early in the morning of March 5, 1951, we
stepped into the Chevrolet (recovered from Shanghai)
for a quiet, unnoticed departure. Standing by were two
close associates, who also later appeared to see us off at
the Hangchow station. On the previous evening, in an in-
conspicuous way, representative staff members and fellowship leaders had gathered for a prayer service and to give
their parting words. They also presented us with a lovely
handmade Chinese-style memory book containing 170 sig-
natures. All was taken care of, including the ordeal of baggage examination, which Grace had attended to. The day
was done. We could "fold [our] tents, like the Arabs, and
as silently steal away."

Before actually obtaining authorization to leave the
country we experienced ten days of processing in Shanghai. Among the requirements was the more highly professional baggage inspection (some precious articles already
had been filched in Hangchow). Also the matter of personal clearance required the obtaining of a Chinese guar-
antor who would make himself legally responsible for any
misdemeanor on our part before crossing the border.
Again, secret surveillance officers no doubt kept an eye on
us. Ultimately, only with the official exit permit issued by

the high Public Security authorities could we leave the country.

Our days became fairly filled by trips to police and other public offices. There were even midnight knocks at our hotel bedroom door and a pair of police admitted by the steward—"Never mind; only routine inspection." For personal relations, relatively free atmosphere still remained in Shanghai. But one had only to look up at the array of terrifying "hate posters" to catch the official mood: "Watch! An enemy might spring forth at any corner." Even so, in the midst of tension, we renewed many a good fellowship with friends (including ex-President Lee). Nor did we miss the chance of having an occasional drink of real coffee at the Chocolate Shop—to the tune of $10,000 a cup (People's Notes).

A surprising experience occurred in a Government office. We were directed to the Office of Intelligence Inspection, to which questionable items went for reference—books, special papers, field glasses, and the like. Here sat a young man, cap setting deeply over his brow and his manner stern. "This may be difficult," we thought. Then, gently laying off his cap and rising from his chair, he teasingly queried, "Now do you know me? I am your student of political science." This changed everything. We rejoiced at finding one of "our own boys" again, and he expressed regret at our leaving China—even wishing for an early return. In this spirit our several problems received full attention, including having field glasses, watches, and gold wedding rings officially sealed against later inspection difficulties. Then again, he was reassuringly at hand for our departure at the railway station and there publicly bade us good-by.

The wearisome three-day journey by rail carried us southeast across three provinces to Canton and finally

Hong Kong. Though we passed through areas never before seen (the railroad having been connected only recently), little of interest emerged. Nor were we edified by the persistent flow of propaganda pouring from the loudspeaker. Other thoughts took sway. Since the southward route had carried us back through Hangchow and across the great bridge by the campus, our minds clung tightly to that last indelible view. Even more impressive loomed the gracious act of the ever-attentive president, who accompanied us back from Shanghai and gave that memorable handshake of unfailing brotherhood.

Ultimately, the Canton–Hong Kong connecting train delivered us at the border of Kowloon, the tiny Lo Wu station being the only link between Hong Kong and Communist China. Slowly, after hours of waiting in the tropical sun and with a sense of unreality, we passed single file through the narrow barbed-wire passageway into a world of different complexion. It was done! Guests of China no more. Sharp feeling of separation. Burden of concern. How much of our hearts had we left behind? Only gradually could eyes and spirits open widely to the stable order and marvelous freedom of life in Hong Kong.

By this time, in the China left behind, all Mission institutions were reaching their deepest crisis. Foreign funds had been cut off; most of the few remaining missionaries were definitely ordered out, leaving several without exit permits. Chinese Christian leaders were grievously harassed. One thought of the colossal tragedy, of the youthful Chinese church being completely isolated from the world Christian brotherhood! Such a peril had already been intimated. Nevertheless, I kept hopefully recalling the touching moment in Shanghai in the company of the general secretary of the Church of Christ in China (also chairman of the Hangchow University Control Board).

Taking my hand, he gave the parting commission: "Go, tell the churches in America that the Church of Christ in China will live. Bid them to hold us close in prayer. And now—God speed."

From the president we received a brief letter in Hong Kong. And later, after returning home via Europe, we received a few veiled missives. Still we could feel that intimate warmth and catch the meaning of those cryptic expressions: "It takes extraordinary eyes to see extraordinary objects. . . . Things are happening here incalculable in time and space. . . . The price of love is always high—to make the best out of the worst at great risk. . . . Remembrance, thought, and feeling radiate universally. . . . We are not really separated, for the Unifying Cross is out there and within us at the same time."

Once on a quiet winter evening he had told us about his boyhood, how out of a family of devout Buddhists he had stepped into the light of the Christian faith. Hence, his mother called him "my lost boy." "Sometime," said he, "I shall write the story of my life, entitling it 'The Boy That Was Lost.'" We shall never return to the China that so possessed our hearts! We shall wait for that China to come to us in the full story of "The Boy That Was Lost."

SELECTED READING

Clayton, Edward H., *Heaven Below*. Prentice-Hall, Inc., 1944.

Clubb, Oliver Edmund, *20th Century China*. Columbia University Press, 1964.

Day, Clarence Burton, *Hangchow University: A Brief History*. United Board for Christian Higher Education in Asia, 1956.

Martin, W. A. P., *The Lore of Cathay*. Fleming H. Revell Company, 1901.

Powell, John B., *My Twenty-five Years in China*. The Macmillan Company, 1945.

Price, Francis W., *China—Twilight or Dawn?* Friendship Press, 1948.

Sturton, Stephen Douglas, *From Mission Hospital to Concentration Camp*. London: Marshall, Morgan & Scott, Ltd., 1948.